D0243629

iDENTIFICATION GUiDES

British & European
Butterflies

Publisher and Creative Director: Nick Wells
Project Editor: Sara Robson
Picture Research: Gemma Walters
Consultant Naturalist: Chris McLaren
Art Director: Mike Spender
Digital Design and Production: Chris Herbert
Layout Design: Basil UK Ltd.

Special thanks to: Chelsea Edwards, Julie Pallot, Sarah Sherman, Helen Tovey and Claire Walker

07 09 11 10 08

1 3 5 7 9 10 8 6 4 2

This edition first published 2007 by
FLAME TREE PUBLISHING
Crabtree Hall, Crabtree Lane
Fulham, London SW6 6TY
United Kingdom

www.flametreepublishing.com

Flame Tree Publishing is part of the Foundry Creative Media Co. Ltd.

ISBN 978-1-84451-841-8

A CIP record for this book is available from the British Library upon request.

Printed in China

IDENTIFICATION GUIDES

British & European
Butterflies

Pamela Forey and Sue McCormick

FLAME TREE
PUBLISHING

Contents

Introduction

There are about 400 butterfly species in Europe, about 60 of them resident in the British Isles. We cannot include all of them in a book this size, but we have selected the most common and widely distributed species for inclusion and designed the book for people who know little about butterflies. The book is simple to use and enables you to identify a butterfly you might see in your garden or on a walk; and gives you some information about it.

How to Use this Book

We have divided the book into sections based on the families of butterflies, since these are relatively clear-cut and easy to distinguish from each other. With very little experience you will begin to spot the various families, and then identifying individual species becomes easier. The families are: **Swallowtails and Apollos; Whites and Yellows; Blues, Coppers and Hairstreaks; Metalmarks; Aristocrats and Fritillaries; Browns; Milkweed Butterflies; Nettle-Tree Butterflies; and Skippers**. If you are already confident you can identify a butterfly as to its family, then you can turn directly to that section, in order to identify it more accurately. If however, you are unsure of the family to which it belongs, then you can use the key in the **Guide to Identification** which follows, to find the right family.

Guide to Identification

Butterflies are insects. Like all insects they have bodies with hard but flexible exoskeletons divided into three sections (head, thorax and abdomen); there are two antennae on the head; and three pairs of legs and two pairs of wings on the thorax.

Butterflies and moths can be distinguished from other insects by their scale-covered wings. And butterflies can be distinguished from moths by their antennae – butterfly antennae are knobbed or clubbed while moth antennae are variable in form but never have knobs or clubs. In general, butterflies are brightly coloured, day-flying insects while moths are dull-coloured, night-flying insects (although there are exceptions to this rule); moths hold their wings flat over the body or in a roof-like position when at rest while butterflies hold their wings vertically. Skippers, although usually considered to be butterflies (they have clubbed antennae), are rather different to the rest, especially in the way they hold their wings.

In this guide we have used differences in the wing colours, antennae and legs to distinguish the butterflies of the various families. Details are also given for eggs, caterpillars and pupae (see Fig. 5 on p.21). Page numbers will enable you to turn directly to the relevant family.

Swallowtails and Apollos (family *Papilionidae*) 22–31

Large butterflies with brightly coloured wings, many (but not all) with a tail on each hind wing. All three pairs of legs fully developed; each leg ends in a single claw. Knob of antennae usually curved. Swallowtails have strong gliding flight, apollos and festoons flutter and flap.

Eggs hemispherical. Caterpillars variable but generally stout with only minute hairs when fully grown. A forked retractable gland just behind the head of the caterpillar can be extruded if it is threatened and produces an offensive scent. Pupae of swallowtails are formed without cocoons and suspended from a pad of silk by a silken girdle; pupae of festoons are attached to a stem by a silken thread at the head, and by the tail; pupae of apollos lie on the ground (often under stones) in loose cocoons.

11 species in Europe, 1 in the British Isles.

Whites and Yellows (family *Pieridae*) 32–71

Medium-sized butterflies with white or yellow wings, often with black veins. (Wing colours come from waste products stored in the wings). All three pairs of legs fully developed; each leg ends in four claws. Males and females often different; spring and summer generations also often different. Knob of antenna straight. Many have a fluttery kind of flight but can nevertheless travel long distances. Several are famous migrants.

Eggs tall, bottle-shaped and ribbed. Caterpillars elongated and cylindrical, often green, with a covering of short hairs and no warts or spines. Pupae are formed without a cocoon but suspended upright from a pad of silk by a silken girdle; the tail end is attached to the silk pad and the head is pointed.

About 40 species in Europe, 6 resident in the British Isles.

Blues, Coppers and Hairstreaks (family *Lycaenidae*)   72–171

Small, often brightly coloured, metallic butterflies. Males very different in colour from females. Males often blue or copper-coloured, females brown. However, both sexes in any one species have similar markings on the undersides of the wings. First two pairs of legs in male slightly smaller than other legs, with only one claw each, otherwise legs fully developed with a pair of claws on each. Antennae have long clubs. Flight rapid but these butterflies do not travel far and often live in local colonies.

Eggs broader than high and disc-like, with rounded edges and a sculptured surface. Caterpillars shaped like woodlice, short and stout with a retractable head, and covered with short hairs. Many have a special gland on the back which produces honey dew. Pupae are also short and stout, formed without a cocoon. They may be attached to a leaf by the tail and with a silken girdle or lie loose among leaves on the ground.

About 100 species in Europe, 16 in the British Isles.

Metalmarks (family *Riodinidae*)   172–75

Most closely related to the blues, coppers and hairstreaks, and sharing many features with members of that family. However, males have only two pairs of functional walking legs, the first pair are much reduced and useless for walking, in the female all three pairs are fully developed.

Eggs small and spherical. Caterpillars short and stout like those of blues, but lack the honey-dew gland. Pupae are also stout, formed without a cocoon and attached to plants by the tail and by a silken girdle.

1 species in Europe including the British Isles (the Duke of Burgundy Fritillary).

Aristocrats and Fritillaries (family *Nymphalidae*)   176–269

Medium-sized to large, brightly coloured and brilliantly marked butterflies, males and females generally similar. First two legs small and held close under the head, so that the butterfly appears to have only four legs; in males the front legs are brush-like with long hair-scales, in females the legs have short hairs. Middle and hind two pairs of legs are fully developed and used for walking. Knob of antenna large, oval and flattened. These butterflies have a powerful flight and some travel long distances; others live in local colonies.

Eggs strongly ribbed, often conical or oval. Caterpillars cylindrical and usually spiny; those that lack spines often have horns behind the head. Pupae are also spiny and formed without a cocoon, suspended only by their tails from silken pads; they do not have a silken girdle.

About 70 species in Europe, 18 in the British Isles.

Browns (family *Satyridae*)   270–335

Mostly medium-sized butterflies, almost all (with the exception of Marbled Whites) some shade of brown, often with orange markings and/or eyespots on the wings. One or two veins in the fore wings are swollen at the base. Males and females usually different, although not strikingly so, and males have sex brands on the fore wings. First two legs similar to those of aristocrats and fritillaries. Middle and hind two pairs of legs are fully developed and used for walking. Knobs of antennae vary from species to species. Flight often erratic and dancing, just over the top of vegetation or ground; these butterflies do not travel long distances.

Eggs often barrel-shaped and ribbed. Caterpillars covered in short downy hairs and spindle-shaped, tapering to a relatively small head and to the tail; the tail is forked into two points. Pupae do not have a cocoon, and either lie unattached on the ground or are suspended from a plant by the tail; they do not have a silken girdle.

About 120 species in Europe, 11 in the British Isles.

Milkweed Butterflies (family *Danaidae*)   336–39

There are no naturally occurring members of this family in Europe, but the Monarch (p.336) has become naturalized in the Canary Islands and is found as an irregular migrant further north in Europe and in the British Isles. It is a large tawny-orange butterfly, with the first pair of legs like that of aristocrats and fritillaries.

Monarch eggs are conical and ribbed. Caterpillar is transversely striped in green, black and yellow. Pupa is stumpy, pale green and suspended by a black thread.

Nettle-Tree Butterflies (family *Libytheidae*)   340–41

Small brown and orange butterflies with characteristic long palps which project from the front of the head like a snout. Fore wings have truncated tips and margins of hind wings are scalloped. In the male, the first pair of legs is reduced like those of aristocrats and fritillaries, and only the middle and hind legs are used for walking; in females all three pairs of legs are fully developed.

Eggs oval and ridged. Caterpillars cylindrical, slightly hairy, green or brown in colour. Pupae are stout, angular and ridged, formed without a cocoon and suspended by the tail only.

1 species in Europe, none in the British Isles.

Skippers (family *Hesperiidae*)

Small orange-brown to dark-grey butterflies with wings different in structure from all other butterflies, in that all the veins arise from the cells and do not branch. Males have sex brands on the fore wings. Skippers have thick moth-like bodies; their broad heads are usually wider than the thorax and bear large, protruding eyes. Antennae have widely separated bases and end in tapering clubs, often pointed and more or less hooked at the tip. All three pairs of legs are fully developed and used for walking; the hind legs in many species bear spurs (like many moths). Flight is rapid and darting, and skippers are often described as skipping from flower to flower.

Eggs variable; they have no form which is characteristic of the family. Caterpillar has a broad head separated from the rest of the body by a constricted 'neck' (actually the constricted first segment); the body tapers at both ends and is sparsely hairy. Caterpillar lives in a shelter formed from leaves or grasses, linked together by silk. Pupae are formed in their leafy shelters, inside silken cocoons.

About 40 species in Europe, 8 in the British Isles.

Types of Butterflies

FIG. 1

15

Swallowtail

Large White

Common Blue

High Brown Fritillary

Meadow Brown

Small Skipper

Making a Positive Identification

At the top of each spread you will find the common and Latin names of the butterfly together with its size, given in the size symbol (see Fig. 2 below) and as an actual measurement of the wingspan (measured from the centre of the thorax along each wing to its tip, not from tip to tip). At the foot of each spread is the time of year at which the butterfly is likely to be seen. Latitude and elevation are critical factors influencing the emergence of butterflies from their pupae, and where a species flies at different times in the northern and southern parts of its range, this has been indicated. Where a butterfly flies in both mountain and lowland areas it usually emerges earlier in the season in the lowlands than in the mountains.

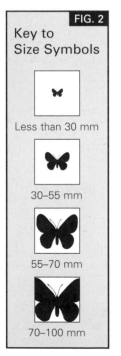

FIG. 2
Key to Size Symbols

Less than 30 mm

30–55 mm

55–70 mm

70–100 mm

On each spread, four paragraphs of text provide details which make positive identification possible (see Fig. 4). The first paragraph, under **Adult Characteristics**, gives information on colour and wing patterns which, together with the illustration, enable you to identify your butterfly. Details of **Habitat and Distribution** are given in the second paragraph (and the distribution is also given in the map in the illustration). The third paragraph, under **Caterpillar Characteristics**, gives you information on the caterpillar and its foodplant. Finally, the fourth paragraph indicates some species with which it might be confused and/or gives some idea of the variation within the species. Those species printed in **bold** are illustrated, either as featured species or in the **Other Common Species** sections; those printed in ordinary type are not.

Distribution Map
- ● Widespread and resident in this area
- ○ Partial distribution only or reaching the limits of its distribution in this area
- ★ Migrates into this area during the summer

FIG. 3

Specimen Spread

Common name of butterfly

Size symbol

Size of butterfly

Colour illustrations
of characteristics

FIG. 4

Latin
name

Colour denotes
family

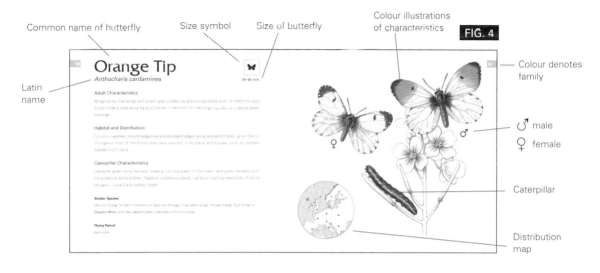

Orange Tip
Anthocharis cardamines

38–48 mm

Adult Characteristics

Wings white, fore wings with a dark grey or black tip and a single black spot. In males this spot is set inside a wide apical band of orange. Undersides of hind wings dappled with yellow-green markings.

Habitat and Distribution

Found in meadows, around hedgerows and woodland edges, along woodland tracks, up to 1500 m. Throughout most of the British Isles, less common in Scotland, and Europe, north to northern Sweden and Finland.

Caterpillar Characteristics

Caterpillar green along the back, shading into blue-green on the sides, dark green beneath, with many black or white bristles. Feeds on cruciferous plants, mainly on ripening seed pods, of plants like garlic mustard and cuckoo flower.

Similar Species

Morocco Orange Tip flies in mountains of Spain and Portugal; it has yellow wings. Female Orange Tip is similar to Dappled White, both have dappled green undersides to the fore wings.

Flying Period

April–June

♂ male

♀ female

Caterpillar

Distribution
map

Orange Tip

Colour
photograph
offering an
alternative
view,
showing the
butterfly in
its typical
habitat.

Other Common Species

At the end of certain groups of butterflies (**Blues** and **Browns** for instance) you will find pages of **Other Common Species**. These are mostly less widespread than the featured butterflies, less likely to be encountered or very similar to one of the featured species.

Now you are ready to use this book. Good luck – and don't forget to tick off your sightings on the checklist provided with the index! Butterflies are among the most beautiful living things in the world, far more beautiful alive and in flight than in a box. Many are endangered by development or changes in land practice, like many other animal and plant species and some are protected species. So please don't collect them, but take a photograph instead!

Life History of a Butterfly

Butterflies, like many other insects, have a complicated life cycle. Males search for females by sight and then court them. Many males produce a pleasant scent from special scales on their fore wings (the scales are often but not always gathered into sex brands), and he scatters his scent around the female as he courts her. After mating, the females lay their eggs on a wide variety of plants, sometimes singly, sometimes in rows or clusters, usually on the undersides of leaves.

The larvae or caterpillars emerge after a few days or may remain in the eggs over the winter to emerge in spring. The caterpillar, as illustrated in Fig. 5 opposite, is quite different to the adult butterfly in form and lifestyle. At first the caterpillar is very small but it grows quickly, feeding on the leaves or flowers of the foodplant on which the eggs were laid. It sheds its skin several times during this period and its appearance may change considerably after each skin change. The descriptions given in the texts refer to the fully grown caterpillar.

Once it reaches its full size it becomes lethargic. At this stage some caterpillars spin a cocoon of silk, but all find a hiding place unique to the species and shed their skin for a final time. The form that emerges is quite different and is called a pupa or chrysalis. Its skin soon hardens and inside radical changes take place in the form of the animal, a process called metamorphosis. At the end of this process the pupa splits open and the adult butterfly emerges.

The adult butterfly has a 'furry' body divided into three parts: the head, thorax and abdomen. Attached to the thorax are two pairs of brightly coloured, scale-covered wings (two fore wings and two hind wings), and three pairs of legs. In its mouth the butterfly has a long, coiled, tubular proboscis which it uses to feed on the nectar of flowers; there are furry palps in front of the proboscis and long clubbed antennae on the top of the head.

Life Cycle of a Butterfly FIG. 5

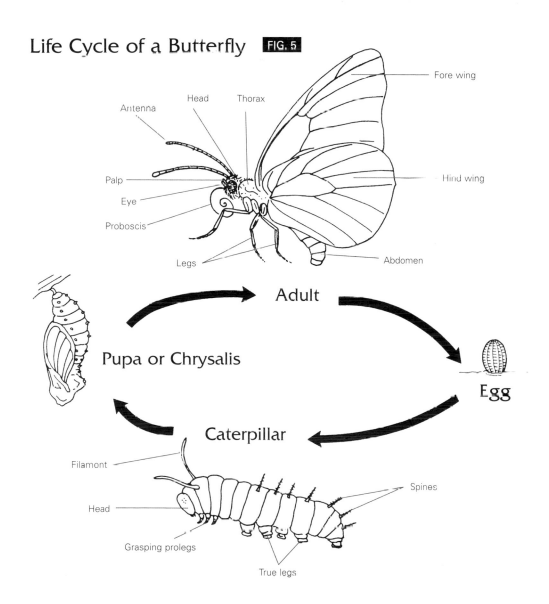

Fore wing

Head   Thorax

Antenna

Palp

Eye

Proboscis

Legs

Hind wing

Abdomen

Adult

Pupa or Chrysalis

Egg

Caterpillar

Filamont

Head

Grasping prolegs

True legs

Spines

Swallowtail

Papilio machaon

64–100 mm

Adult Characteristics

Wings yellow with dense black markings; broad black border with yellow spots on back of fore wings. Broad black border on back of hind wings contains blurred blue spots and yellow crescents. Hind wings tailed, with single red spot at base.

Habitat and Distribution

Found in meadows and flowery grassy places, from lowlands to mountains up to about 2000 m. Throughout continental Europe but becoming more rare than formerly in the central countries. Confined to the Norfolk Broads in Britain. Protected.

Caterpillar Characteristics

Caterpillar green, striped with black and orange. It protrudes a pair of orange horns if startled. Feeds mainly on umbelliferous plants like milk parsley, wild carrot and fennel.

Similar Species

Southern Festoon flies in lowland meadows of southern Europe, Spanish Festoon in hills and mountains. Both have yellow wings with black bands, red spots and zig-zag-like black borders.

Flying Period

April–May & July–August (S); May–July (N & GB).

Due to the declining numbers of Swallowtail butterflies, they are now a protected species.

Scarce Swallowtail
Iphiclides podalirius

65–90 mm

Adult Characteristics

Wings pale creamy yellow, with six dark vertical stripes on each fore wing. Hind wings have a black border along the rear edges, studded with blue crescent-shaped spots and with a single red crescent above innermost blue spot. Hind wings have long tails.

Habitat and Distribution

Found in gardens and hedges, woods and orchards in lowland areas of Europe, from the Mediterranean to Belgium and Germany. Occasional vagrants reach the North and Baltic Seas or cross the Channel into southern England. Protected.

Caterpillar Characteristics

Caterpillar green with a yellow stripe along the back and oblique yellow side stripes. Feeds on hawthorn, sloe, cherries and other fruit trees.

Similar Species

Southern Swallowtail has bright yellow wings and four stripes on fore wings; it is found in foothills of Alps, especially on western slopes.

Flying Period

April–June & August–September.

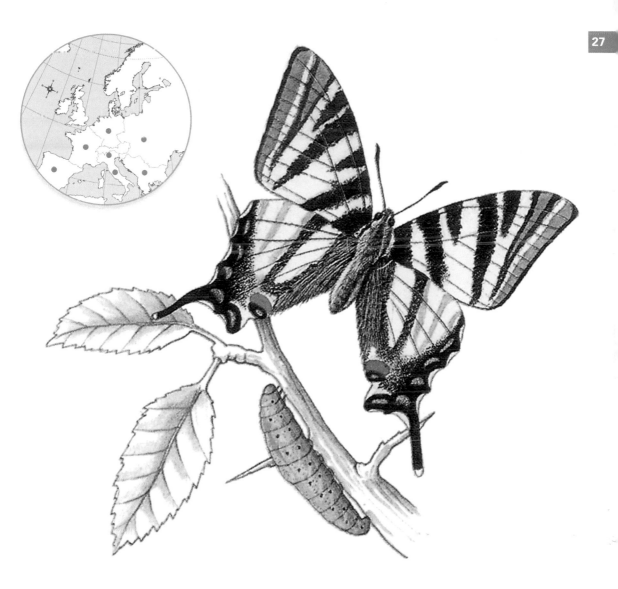

Apollo
Parnassius apollo

70–85 mm

Adult Characteristics

Wings of male white, of female greyish. Both sexes have two large black spots and several smaller ones in the fore wings; hind wings have two black-bordered, red spots, often with white centres to the spots. Other spots may also be present.

Habitat and Distribution

Found in mountains from southern Spain, Sicily and Turkey to Scandinavia, at altitudes of 700–1800 m in the south, lower in the north. Most often in valleys and meadows. Absent from Britain. Rare in some areas of central Europe. Protected.

Caterpillar Characteristics

Caterpillar velvety black with short black hairs growing from raised warts, and red spots along the sides. Feeds on various species of stonecrops and houseleeks.

Similar Species

Clouded Apollo flies in mountain meadows in central Europe; it has no red spots, only two black spots on fore wings. Small Apollo (with many red spots) is confined to the Alps.

Flying Period

July–September.

The Apollo butterfly is found primarily in the mountainous regions of southern Spain, Sicily and Turkey.

Black-Veined White

Aporia crataegi

55–68 mm

Adult Characteristics

Wings white. Males have dark-brown or black veins and some black scales on the undersides of the wings. Females larger, with brown veins and few scales on the wings so that they look almost transparent.

Habitat and Distribution

Found in open woodland and clearings, orchards and open country from sea level to 1800 m, throughout continental Europe, north to central Scandinavia and Finland. The species became extinct in Britain in the 1920s.

Caterpillar Characteristics

Caterpillar malodorous, with poisonous hairs, brownish or grey with wide black band on back and two rusty side stripes. Feeds in groups in silken webs, on hawthorn, plum, blackthorn and other *Prunus* species and at one time were pests in orchards.

Similar Species

Clouded Apollo has black spots on wings. Dark-Veined White is a form of the **Green-Veined White** found in the mountains; males have black veins on the upper sides of the wings.

Flying Period

May–July.

The Black-Veined White is a striking species that has been extinct in Britain since the 1920s, but is still to be found on the Continent.

Large White
Pieris brassicae

55–65 mm

Adult Characteristics

Wings white or yellowish with black tips and a black mark on front edge of hind wing. Undersides of hind wings and tips of fore wings yellow or grey. Females have two black spots and a black streak on fore wing; males have no spots on upper side but two black spots on underside of fore wing.

Habitat and Distribution

Common in gardens, found in many other places, from lowlands to 1800 m throughout Europe and the British Isles, north to central Scandinavia and Finland. Many individuals migrate long distances.

Caterpillar Characteristics

Caterpillars are notorious pests on cabbages and other brassicas, feeding in groups and making large holes in the leaves. They are grey-green with yellow and black markings and short white hairs. They smell unpleasant.

Similar Species

Small White is smaller and has much smaller, less well-defined markings.

Flying Period

April–May & July–August, also September–October.

The caterpillars of the Large Whites make their mark on many European gardens by devouring cabbages and other vegetables.

Small White
Artogeia rapae

45–55 mm

Adult Characteristics

Wings white or yellowish with dark tips; underside of fore wings white with a yellow tip and two black spots on each, of hind wings yellow. Male has one small grey or black spot on fore wing, female has two small spots and a dash.

Habitat and Distribution

Found in gardens, meadows, roadsides and many other places, from sea level to 1800 m, throughout the British Isles and Europe, north to central Scandinavia and Finland. One of the most common butterflies. Many migrate long distances.

Caterpillar Characteristics

Caterpillars are pests on cabbages and other brassicas, feeding singly on many cruciferous plants in the wild. They are greenish with a yellow stripe along the back, a row of yellow spots along the sides and many white hairs.

Similar Species

Two other small whites, Southern Small White and Mountain Small White, fly in rough rocky places in southern Europe. **Large White** is much larger, with larger spots.

Flying Period

March–May & June–September/October.

The Small White is one of the most common butterflies throughout Europe, migrating even as far as Finland.

Green-Veined White

Artogeia napi

35–50 mm

Adult Characteristics

Undersides of hind wings yellow, with veins picked out in grey or greenish scales. Some summer forms lack this veining. Upper sides of wings white or yellowish with grey or black veins and a dark tip, one black spot on fore wings in males, at least two in females.

Habitat and Distribution

Found in open countryside, often near water, in damp meadows and open woodland, along woodland margins, from marshland to mountain valleys, from sea level to over 2500 m. Throughout Europe and the British Isles.

Caterpillar Characteristics

Caterpillar green with yellow rings around the spiracles, and covered with short white hairs. Feeds on wild crucifers, charlock, watercress etc., but rarely on garden brassicas.

Similar Species

Dark-Veined White is a form that occurs in the mountains; males have black veins on the upper sides of the wings.

Large White has yellow underside to the hind wings, without the grey veins.

Flying Period

March–June & July–September.

Some summer forms of the Green-Veined White do not have the veins marked in grey or greenish scales.

Dappled White
Euchloe simplonia

40–48 mm

Adult Characteristics

Fore wings creamy white with patchy black and white tips and a central black spot; hind wings white. Undersides of hind wings and tips of fore wings dappled with green markings, dense green in spring brood, paler and yellow-green in summer brood.

Habitat and Distribution

Found in open meadows and on hillsides to 1400 m in southern Europe, from Portugal and Spain, through southern France and Italy, to the Balkans and Turkey.

Caterpillar Characteristics

Caterpillar pale blue-green with black spots; a dark grey-green, yellow-edged stripe runs along the back; a white stripe runs along each side, bordered with yellow on its lower side. Feeds on cruciferous plants, like candytuft and wild radish.

Similar Species

Several similar species occur in southern Europe, like Mountain Dappled White, found high in Alps and Pyrenees. Hind wing of **Bath White** has one black spot in male, many in female.

Flying Period

March–April & May–June.

Bath White

Pontia daplidice

42–48 mm

Adult Characteristics

Fore wings white with dappled black tips and a central black spot, females more heavily marked than males. Hind wings mainly white in males, with black markings in females. Undersides of hind wings and tips of fore wings mainly green with white spots.

Habitat and Distribution

Found in meadows, fields and rough ground in central and southern Europe, north to France and Germany. Many individuals migrate long distances, occasional vagrants fly further north and to England, rarely Norway and Ireland.

Caterpillar Characteristics

Caterpillar grey-mauve with two yellow stripes on each side, yellow spots above prolegs, many black spots and white hairs. Feeds on mignonettes and cruciferous plants, especially mustards.

Similar Species

Undersides of hind wings and fore-wing tips mainly olive-green in spring brood, yellow-green in summer brood.

Dappled White is confined to southern Europe and has white hind wings.

Flying Period

February–March, April–May & July–August.

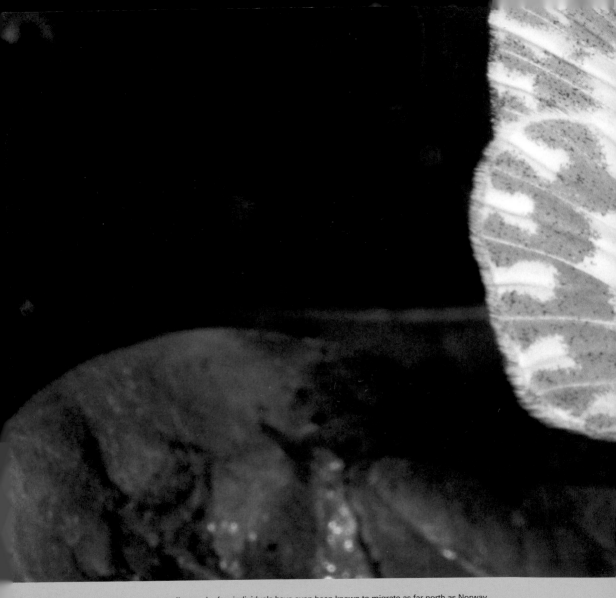
Bath Whites are known as great travellers and a few individuals have even been known to migrate as far north as Norway.

Orange Tip
Anthocharis cardamines

38–48 mm

Adult Characteristics

Wings white, fore wings with a dark-grey or black tip and a single black spot. In males this spot is just inside a wide apical band of orange. Undersides of hind wings dappled with yellow-green markings.

Habitat and Distribution

Found in meadows, around hedgerows and woodland edges, along woodland tracks, up to 1500 m. Throughout most of the British Isles (less common in Scotland) and Europe, north to northern Sweden and Finland.

Caterpillar Characteristics

Caterpillar green along the back, shading into blue-green on the sides, dark green beneath, with many black or white bristles. Feeds on cruciferous plants, mainly on ripening seed pods, of plants like garlic mustard and cuckoo flower.

Similar Species

Morocco Orange Tip flies in mountains of Spain and Portugal; it has yellow wings. Female Orange Tip is similar to **Dappled White**; both have dappled green undersides to the hind wings.

Flying Period

April–June.

♀

♂

Orange Tips are noted for the attractive dappled undersides of their hind wings.

Wood White
Leptidea sinapis

35–48 mm

Adult Characteristics

A small butterfly with creamy white wings. Tips of fore wings are grey in spring brood, grey in females and black in males in summer brood. Undersides of wings also creamy white, suffused with yellow-grey on hind wings and parts of fore wings.

Habitat and Distribution

Found in glades and rides in open woodland, throughout much of Europe, north to northern Scandinavia and Finland. Also from central and southern England to south Wales and Ireland. Recognizable from its weak fluttering flight.

Caterpillar Characteristics

Caterpillar green with a dark line along the back and a yellow stripe on each side. Feeds on members of the pea family including bird's-foot trefoil, meadow vetchling and vetches.

Similar Species

Two similar wood whites occur in Europe. Eastern Wood White flies in Alps and mountains of southeastern Europe. Fenton's Wood White flies in lowland areas of central-eastern Europe.

Flying Period

May–June & July–August (S).

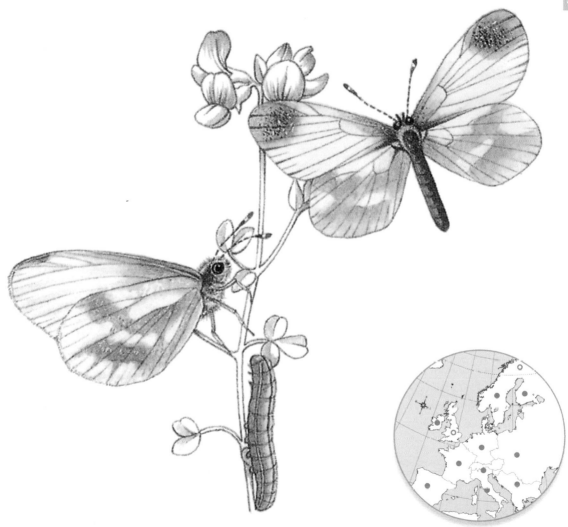

Interestingly the spring brood and female Wood Whites have grey tips on their fore wings, but the male summer brood have black tips.

Brimstone

Gonepteryx rhamni

50–70 mm

Adult Characteristics

Fore wings hooked, hind wings with blunt tails. Males have sulphur-yellow wings, females greenish-white wings; both have an orange spot on each wing.

Habitat and Distribution

Found in open places and woodland, wandering all over Europe, the southern half of Britain and all Ireland. They live for up to a year, hatching in summer and flying until autumn, then hibernating. Spring butterflies have emerged from hibernation.

Caterpillar Characteristics

Caterpillar blue-green with black speckles on its back, with a white stripe along each side, and yellow-green beneath. Feeds on leaves of buckthorn.

Similar Species

The Cleopatra is a very similar butterfly found in Mediterranean Europe; however the hind wing tails may be almost non-existent and the males have orange fore wings.

Flying Period

April–May & June–September.

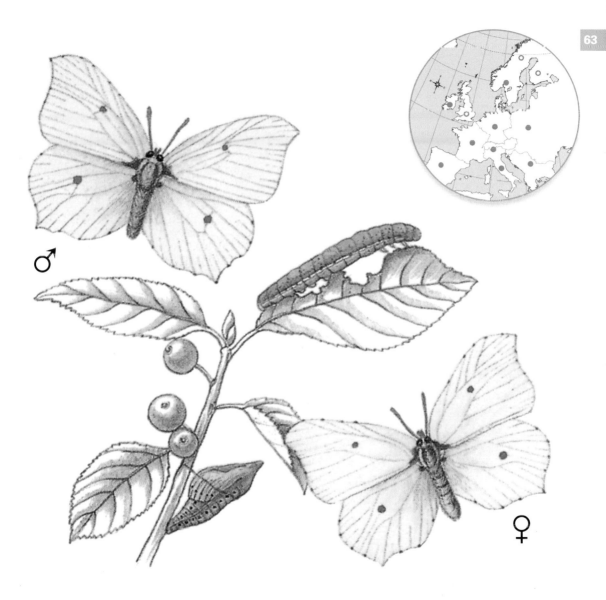

♂

♀

The attractive hood-winged Brimstone butterflies can live for up to a year.

Clouded Yellow
Colias crocea

46–54 mm

Adult Characteristics

Wings bright orange-yellow with black borders, and one round black spot on each fore wing. Undersides have dark spots on fore wing and a silver spot on hind wing. In females the black borders contain yellow spots; some females have pale creamy wings.

Habitat and Distribution

A famous migrant butterfly. Resident in central and southern Europe, in open places and heaths to 1800 m, but migrating to northern Europe and Britain, in occasional years in thousands. In a bad year only a few individuals migrate north.

Caterpillar Characteristics

Caterpillar velvety green with many black spots, each with a single white hair. Yellowish line with orange-red dashes runs along each side. Feeds on members of the pea family, especially on clovers and lucerne, but also on bird's-foot trefoil.

Similar Species

One of over 10 Clouded Yellows in Europe. Most males have paler wings, e.g. sulphur-coloured Moorland Clouded Yellow, found in moors and bogs in northern Europe. Females often white.

Flying Period

April–May & July–October.

In a good year thousands of Clouded Yellows migrate to northern Europe and Britain; a bad year, however, sees only sporadic migrants.

Pale Clouded Yellow

Colias hyale

42–50 mm

Adult Characteristics

Wings of male pale yellow, of female white tinted with yellow-green. Both have black, white-blotched borders and red fringes, an oval black spot on the fore wing and an orange spot on the hind wing.

Habitat and Distribution

Another famous migrant. Resident, common in some years and scarce in others, in central Europe north of the Pyrenees, in meadows, lucerne and clover fields to over 1800 m. They migrate north, in large numbers in some years, occasionally to Britain.

Caterpillar Characteristics

Caterpillar velvety green with an orange and yellow-white stripe along each side, and many short black hairs. Feeds on lucerne, vetches and other plants in the pea family.

Similar Species

Berger's Clouded Yellows often fly with Pale Clouded Yellows. Their females are difficult to distinguish but male Bergers have brighter yellow wings with less extensive black markings.

Flying Period

May–June & August–September.

Long-Tailed Blue
Lampides boeticus

30–36 mm

Adult Characteristics

Wings of male violet-blue and hairy with a narrow dark border; of female brown towards the edges, blue in the centre. Both sexes have tailed hind wings. Undersides beige with transverse creamy stripes, on the hind wing one stripe wider than the others. There are dark spots near the tail.

Habitat and Distribution

Found in rough places, flowery meadows and fields, from lowlands to 2000 m. Resident in southern Europe but migrating north each year, reaching France, Belgium and Germany by late summer, occasionally crossing the Channel to southern England.

Caterpillar Characteristics

Caterpillar short and stout, varying in colour from dark green to reddish-brown, with a dark stripe along the back and oblique stripes on the sides. It feeds on pods of various leguminous plants, especially bladder senna but also peas.

Similar Species

Lang's Short-Tailed Blue is smaller and has a beige and white striped pattern on the undersides without one stripe larger than others. Found in lowland grassland in southern Europe.

Flying Period

May–September.

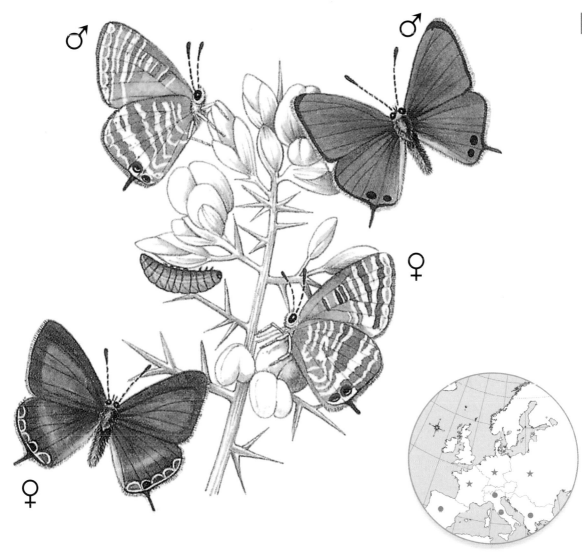

The southern European Long-Tailed Blue migrates north each year, occasionally reaching Britain.

Short-Tailed Blue

Everes argiades

20–30 mm

Adult Characteristics

Wings of male violet-blue with a narrow dark border; of female dark brown, slightly suffused with blue. Both sexes have tailed hind wings; undersides of wings pale grey with lines of small black spots and orange spots near the edge of the hind wing.

Habitat and Distribution

Found in rough lowland grassland, meadows and heaths, often in damp places. Central and southern Europe from the Pyrenees to northern France and east to Greece; occasionally found further north and in Britain. Absent from central and southern Spain.

Caterpillar Characteristics

Caterpillar short and stout, pale green with a darker stripe along the back and pale oblique stripes along the sides. It feeds on pods and leaves of leguminous plants, including medicks, bird's-foot trefoil and gorse.

Similar Species

Provençal Short-Tailed Blue is similar but has no orange spots; it is scattered through southern Europe. **Small Blue** and **Silver-Studded Blue** lack tails.

Flying Period

April–September.

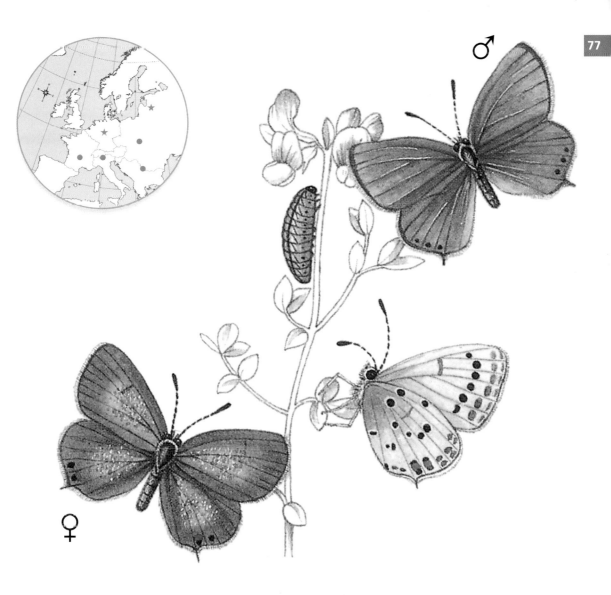

Holly Blue
Celastrina argiolus

26–34 mm

Adult Characteristics

Wings of male sky blue, with a very narrow black border on fore wings. Wings of female darker blue with broad black borders on wings and six black spots on each hind wing. Undersides of both sexes pale blue-white with lines of black spots.

Habitat and Distribution

Found in open woodland, gardens and parks, females around holly or ivy, throughout much of Europe except north-west Scandinavia, in England, Wales and Ireland, most commonly in the south.

Caterpillar Characteristics

Caterpillar resembles a woodlouse with a hump, and is green, most often with an indefinite yellow stripe along the sides, but sometimes with maroon or rose-pink stripes. Feeds on holly and ivy, usually spring brood on holly and summer brood on ivy.

Similar Species

Small Blue has similar underside but is much smaller, with dark upper surface to its wings. Female may be mistaken for **Large Blue** but this has darker grey-brown underside.

Flying Period

April–May & July–August.

Both the male and female Holly Blue has pale-blue undersides, marked with black spots.

Green-Underside Blue

Glaucopsyche alexis

26–36 mm

Adult Characteristics

Wings of male purple-blue with narrow black borders, of females brown suffused with blue. Undersides pale grey flushed with green on the hind wings, and a line of large white-ringed black spots on the fore wings. There may be a few small spots on the hind wings.

Habitat and Distribution

Found around woodland edges or dry meadows, in hills and mountains up to 1200 m. Western and northern Europe, from northern Spain to southern Scandinavia and Finland, more common in the south. Absent from Britain, northern Germany and Denmark.

Caterpillar Characteristics

Caterpillar short and stout, shaggy, green or brown with a red-brown line along its back and red-brown oblique stripes on its sides. It feeds on various leguminous plants, including milk vetches and broom.

Similar Species

Black-Eyed Blue is similar; it is found around broom plants in Spain.

Large Blue has many black spots on the underside and a line of black spots on the upper surface of its fore wings.

Flying Period

April–June.

Alcon Blue

Maculinea alcon

34–38 mm

Adult Characteristics

Wings of male pale dull blue with narrow black borders, of female grey-brown, sometimes flushed with blue at wing bases and/or with indistinct spots. Undersides light brown with lines of white-ringed, black spots.

Habitat and Distribution

Found in marshy places and damp meadows from lowlands to 900 m, locally in central Europe from France eastwards, south to the Alps and northern Spain, north to Germany and southern Sweden. Absent from Britain.

Caterpillar Characteristics

Caterpillar green or reddish-brown. Young caterpillars feed on gentian flowers but after the third moult they are carried into ants' nests by the ants and complete their development in the nest, overwintering there and pupating in the spring.

Similar Species

A mountain form flies in alpine meadows and slopes up to 1800 m, in the Pyrenees and Alps for instance. Its wings are brighter blue and slightly flushed with green on the underside.

Flying Period

July.

Large Blue
Maculinea arion

32–42 mm

Adult Characteristics

Wings bright blue with broad black borders and a series of long black spots on each fore wing; spots larger in female than male. Underside grey to grey-brown, flushed with iridescent green at base of hind wings, and with lines of white-ringed black spots.

Habitat and Distribution

Found in rough grassy places up to 1800 m where wild thyme and ants' nests are present. Northern Spain to southern Sweden and east to the Balkans and Greece. Became extinct in Britain in 1979, now reintroduced in one or two places and protected.

Caterpillar Characteristics

Caterpillar short and stout, pale pink with white stripes at first, feeding on thyme flowers. Mature caterpillar falls to ground and produces honeydew; it becomes white and swollen and is taken by a *Myrmica* ant to its nest where it pupates.

Similar Species

Male **Alcon Blue** has no spots on upper sides of wings, female has wings suffused grey-brown. Much rarer Scarce Large Blue and Dusky Large Blue fly in wet meadows in central Europe.

Flying Period

June–July.

The caterpillar of the Large Blue is taken by a *Myrmica* ant to its nest, where it pupates.

Silver-Studded Blue

Plebejus argus

24–34 mm

Adult Characteristics

Wings of male bright mauve-blue with narrow dark-brown borders; of female dark brown slightly flushed with blue and with orange crescents on both wings. Undersides of male grey, of female grey-brown; marginal orange crescents have blue-centred, dark spots to the outside.

Habitat and Distribution

Found in grassy places, heaths and downs, hills and mountains scattered throughout Europe north to northern Scandinavia. In Britain it is now mainly found in southern and eastern England and in western Wales.

Caterpillar Characteristics

Caterpillar short and stout, shaped like a woodlouse, green or brown, with a white-bordered, dark-brown stripe along the back and a white stripe on each side. Feeds on gorse, heather or bird's-foot trefoil. Attended by ants.

Similar Species

Idas Blue is slightly larger and often has a band of orange on hind wings; it is absent from Britain and Iberia.

Common Blue has no blue in the orange and black spots on the undersides.

Flying Period

May–August.

In Britain, the Silver-Studded Blue can be found primarily in southern and eastern England and western Wales.

Idas Blue
Lycaeides idas

28–34 mm

Adult Characteristics

Wings of male bright blue with narrow black border; of female brown, with brown crescents especially on hind wings, and often blue at the base. Undersides grey or yellow-grey with many black spots and blue-centred, orange marginal spots often forming a wide band.

Habitat and Distribution

Found in sandy heathland, rough places and mountain slopes up to 1500 m, throughout most of Europe. Absent from southern Spain and Portugal and from Britain.

Caterpillar Characteristics

Caterpillar short and stout, green or brown with a dark red-brown, white-edged stripe along each flank and white stripes on its sides. At first it feeds on leguminous plants or buckthorn, but mature caterpillars are taken by ants to their nests to overwinter.

Similar Species

Silver-Studded Blue is very similar but is generally smaller; its orange crescents have blue-centred black spots to the outside.

Flying Period

June–July.

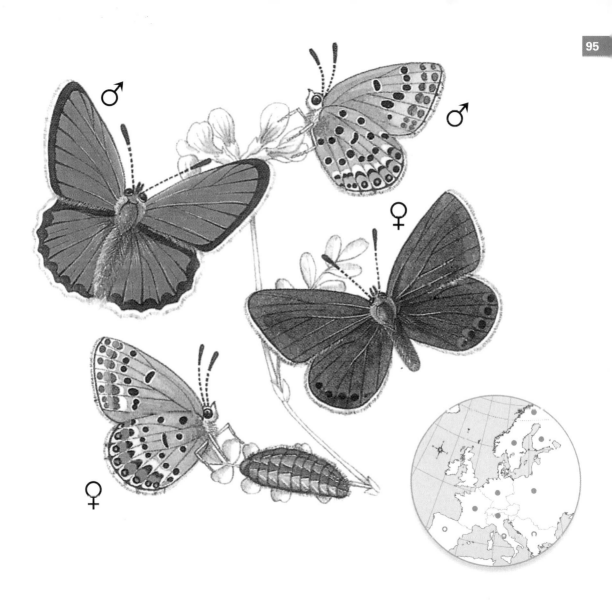

Mature caterpillars of the Idas Blue are carried by ants to their nests, where they overwinter.

Amanda's Blue

Agrodiaetus amanda

30–38 mm

Adult Characteristics

Wings of male blue with dusky brown margins; of female brown, often flushed with blue and with orange crescents on hind wings. Underside of male dove grey, of female grey-brown, both with white-ringed black spots and a row of black-edged orange spots.

Habitat and Distribution

Found in dry meadows and hillsides up to 1500 m, local but widely distributed across southern Europe from northern Spain to Balkans and through eastern Europe to Scandinavia. Absent from northwest Europe, including Britain, France and Germany.

Caterpillar Characteristics

Caterpillar green with long pale hairs; it has a dark-green, light-edged stripe on its back and a yellowish stripe on each side. Its head is hidden from above by the swollen front segments. It feeds on tufted vetch and is tended by ants.

Similar Species

Damon Blue has wide dusky margins to pale shining blue wings, and yellow-grey undersides with a white streak in middle of hind wing. It flies in mountains in continental Europe.

Flying Period

June–August.

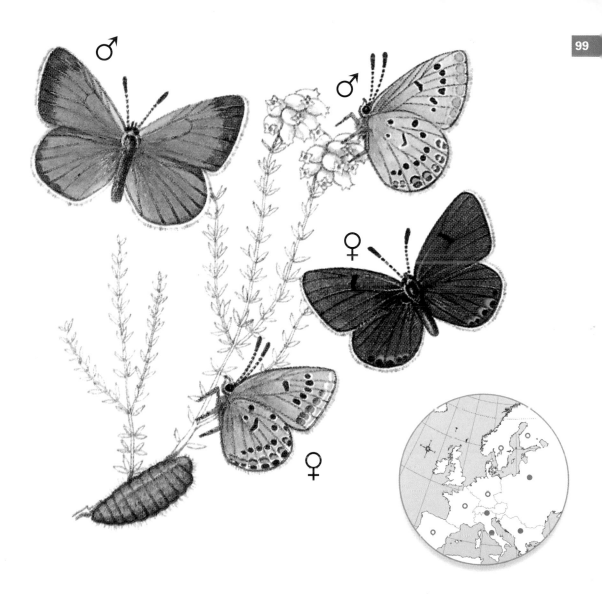

The Amanda's Blue shown here is the male, the female is brown with orange crescents on its hind wings.

Chalk-Hill Blue

Lysandra coridon

30–36 mm

Adult Characteristics

Wings of male pale silver-blue with narrow black border on fore wings, breaking into black spots on hind wings; of female dark brown with black-centred orange spots on hind wings. Underside of male pale grey, of female brown, both with white-ringed black spots, the outer ones edged with orange crescents.

Habitat and Distribution

Found in chalk and limestone grassland from sea level to 1800 m. Northern Spain to the Baltic coast in Germany and eastward to the Balkans. Also found in southern England. Absent from the rest of Britain and Denmark.

Caterpillar Characteristics

Caterpillar resembles a bright-green woodlouse with a hump; it has yellow stripes on back and sides. It feeds at night on horseshoe vetch in Britain, on this and other small leguminous plants in Europe. Full-grown in June. Tended by ants.

Similar Species

Adonis Blue females are similar to Chalk-Hill Blue females but the orange crescents on their hind wings are edged with blue instead of white.

Flying Period

July–August.

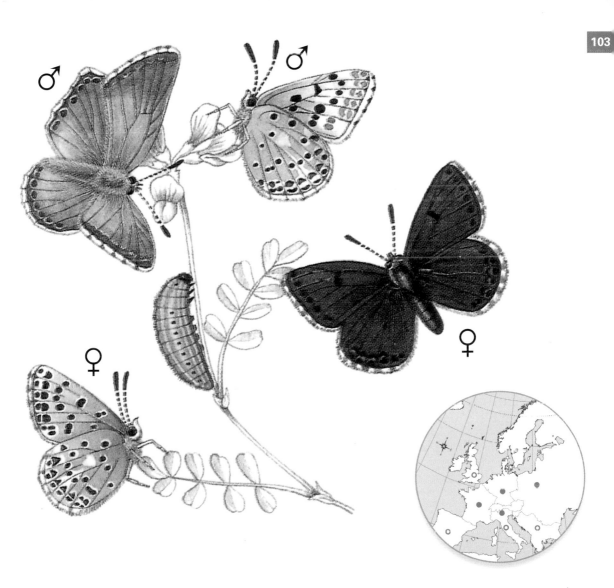

Unsurprisingly, the Chalk-Hill Blue enjoys chalk and limestone areas, from sea level up to altitudes of 1800 m, particularly in western Europe.

Adonis Blue

Lysandra bellargus

28–36 mm

Adult Characteristics

Wings of male vivid sky blue with fine black line on margins; of female dark brown with orange, blue and black spots on hind wings. Underside pale grey-brown in male, darker in female, with white-ringed black spots and a marginal row of orange spots edged with black and white.

Habitat and Distribution

Found in small colonies in open chalk downs with short turf. Southern and central Europe from Portugal and Spain to the Balkans and north to France and Poland, also in southern England but now rare. Absent from Scandinavia.

Caterpillar Characteristics

Caterpillar shaped like a woodlouse with a hump, dark green with yellow stripes along back and sides, very similar to that of Chalk-Hill Blue but full-grown in April and July. Feeds by day on horseshoe vetch or other small legumes. Tended by ants.

Similar Species

Chalk-Hill Blue females are similar but have no blue in the spots on their hind wings. **Common Blue** males have pale violet-blue wings and darker undersides flushed with blue.

Flying Period

May–June & July–September.

This handsome male Adonis Blue lives up to his name, with his striking blue wings and smart black edging.

Common Blue

Polyommatus icarus

28–36 mm

Adult Characteristics

Wings of male pale violet-blue; of female brown, variably flushed with violet-blue, and with orange crescents edged with black. Underside of male grey-beige, of female brown, both flushed with blue, with white-ringed black spots and a row of marginal black spots edged with orange and white crescents.

Habitat and Distribution

Found in grassland, meadows and grassy dunes, roadside verges and waste places, in woodland clearings and heathland, from sea level to 2000 m. Common throughout Europe and the British Isles.

Caterpillar Characteristics

Caterpillar short and stout with an arched back, dark green with a darker line along the back and a paler line along each side. It feeds on small leguminous plants, including bird's-foot trefoil, restharrow and white clover. Tended by ants.

Similar Species

Adonis Blue male has sky-blue wings and paler grey undersides. Common Blue females with no blue on wings resemble **Brown Argus** females; with blue, they resemble **Adonis Blue** females.

Flying Period

April–September.

The male Common Blue is a violet-blue colour; the female is brown shot with blue and has orange and black crescent markings.

Baton Blue
Pseudophilotes baton

20–25 mm

Adult Characteristics

Wings of male powder blue with a narrow black border and a long black spot on each fore wing; of female dark brown flushed with blue at the base. Underside of both sexes pale grey to grey-brown with lines of prominent black spots and black-edged orange crescents along the margin of each hind wing.

Habitat and Distribution

Found in dry grassy places with thyme plants, up to 2000 m but not common. Central Europe from northern Spain and Portugal to northern France and east to Poland. Absent from Britain, Holland, much of Germany, Denmark and Scandinavia.

Caterpillar Characteristics

Caterpillar short, stout and warty in appearance, dark green with wine-red and white stripes on back and sides and white hairs. First brood caterpillars feed on wild thyme, second brood feed on mint, savory and lavender. Tended by ants.

Similar Species

Panoptes Blue and False Baton Blue are related butterflies found in central and southern Spain; they have no orange crescents on the underside of the hind wings.

Flying Period

April–June & July–September.

Small Blue

Cupido minimus

16–24 mm

Adult Characteristics

Very small butterflies with dark-brown wings. Males have a covering of silver-blue scales on their wings, especially near the wing bases. Undersides pale grey, tinged with yellow in females, with lines of white-ringed, black spots in both sexes.

Habitat and Distribution

Found in chalk and limestone grassland, in quarries and woodland rides, on roadsides and cliffs, from sea level to 2000 m. Northern Spain to the coasts of Scandinavia. Local in Britain and Ireland, mainly in southern England.

Caterpillar Characteristics

Caterpillar short and stout, like a woodlouse with a hump, pale yellow-brown with a whitish stripe along each side. It feeds only on kidney vetch in Britain, on this and other small leguminous plants in Europe.

Similar Species

Short-Tailed Blue is similar on the underside and females are brown but its hind wings have short tails.

Flying Period

May–August.

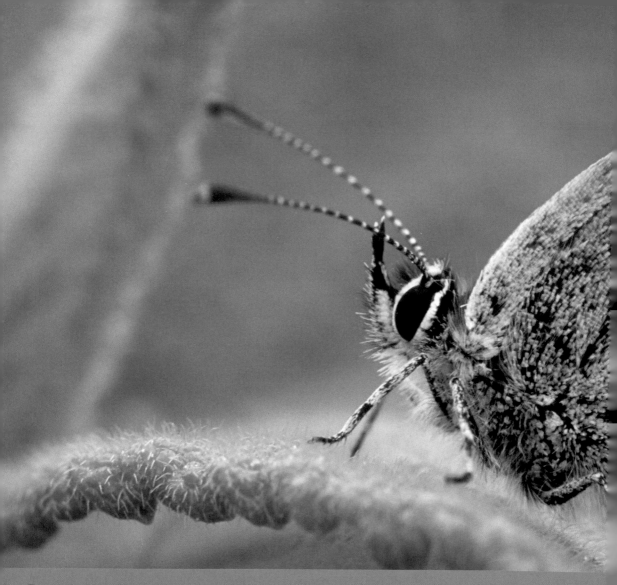

The dainty Small Blue has a caterpillar that resembles a woodlouse, with a hump and a whitish side stripe.

Brown Argus

Aricia agestis

22–28 mm

Adult Characteristics

Wings dark brown with a marginal row of orange crescents, larger in the female. Underside pale grey-brown with lines of white-ringed, dark-brown spots, and a row of white spots towards the edge, each enclosing an orange crescent and a brown spot.

Habitat and Distribution

Found in chalk and limestone grassland, heathland, coastal cliffs and dunes, from sea level to 900 m. Found throughout Europe north to southern Scandinavia and Britain (England and Wales).

Caterpillar Characteristics

Caterpillar shaped like a woodlouse, pale green with discontinuous purple stripes along back and sides. It feeds on rockrose, stork's-bill or dove's-foot cranesbill. Usually found in the company of ants.

Similar Species

May be confused with females of more typical blues. Northern Brown Argus flies in mountains in southern Europe (southern form), in moorland in the north and Scotland (northern form).

Flying Period

April–September.

The orange crescent markings of the Brown Argus are larger on the female, than on the male.

Geranium Argus

Eumedonia eumedon

28–32 mm

Adult Characteristics

Wings dark brown, unmarked in male, with a few orange crescents on hind wings in female. Underside grey to grey-brown, flushed with blue at base of hind wing; with white-ringed black spots, a white streak in the middle and variable orange crescents on hind wings, larger on females.

Habitat and Distribution

Found in meadows, in hills and mountains up to 2400 m, from northern Spain to the Balkans, and north through eastern Europe to eastern Scandinavia and Finland. Absent from northwest Europe, including Britain, France, Germany and Denmark.

Caterpillar Characteristics

Caterpillar green with a yellow stripe along its back, and white and yellow stripes on the sides. It has a black head covered with yellowish hairs. It feeds on crane's-bills.

Similar Species

Northern Brown Argus has well-developed orange crescents on the upper sides of its wings; the northern form has a single white spot on each fore wing.

Flying Period

June–July.

Other Blues

Chequered Blue

Wingspan: 22–28 mm. Northern form (found in southern Scandinavia and Finland) has dull blue wings with grey margins and chequered black and white borders. Southern form (found from northern Spain across central and southern Europe to Greece) has very dark wings with little blue (male) or black wings (female). Underside of both forms white with large black spots and an orange band on margin of hind wing. Found in rough dry places. Flies June–July. Caterpillars feed on stonecrops.

Other Blues

Mazarine Blue

Wingspan: 25–34 mm. Wings of male dull violet-blue with black borders; of female brown. Underside of both sexes light brown flushed with blue, and with a line of white-ringed black spots. Found in lowland and mountain meadows up to 1800 m. Widespread across Europe from northern Spain to Greece and north to Scandinavia; rare in southern Spain and Portugal, extinct in Britain. Flies June–August. Caterpillar feeds on thrift, kidney vetch and clovers.

The Chequered Blue enjoys a variety of habitats, ranging from open woodland and mud flats to sand dunes.

Other Blues

Turquoise Blue

Wingspan: 30–44 mm. Wings of male brilliant pale blue with narrow black margins; of female brown with orange crescents on hind wings. Undersides pale grey with broad white margins and lines of white-ringed black spots. Found locally in mountain meadows and slopes from 900–1500 m in mountain areas of southern and central Europe from northern Spain to the Balkans. Flies May–July and August–September. Caterpillar feeds on melilot, kidney vetch, clover and thyme.

Other Blues

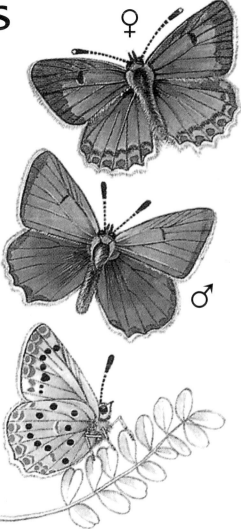

Meleager's Blue

Wingspan: 30–38 mm. Hind wings have scalloped margins. Wings brilliant blue with black margins, darker blue in female than male with wider margins. Underside of male pale grey, of female light brown, both with white-ringed black spots and grey markings around margin. Found on slopes of limestone hills and downs from lowlands to 1300 m. Northeastern Spain and southern France, through hills and mountains of southern Europe eastwards. Flies June. Caterpillar feeds on sainfoin, milkvetch and other legumes.

Brown Hairstreak
Thecla betulae

34–36 mm

Adult Characteristics

Wings brown with small tails on hind wings and orange-red patches on either side of the tails; females have a broad orange-red transverse band on fore wing. Undersides of wings orange-yellow with transverse darker orange band bordered by white stripes.

Habitat and Distribution

Found around hedgerows and woodland edges, males high in trees (often oak or ash), females around blackthorn bushes laying eggs. Throughout much of Europe, England and southern Ireland. Absent from Mediterranean area and much of Scandinavia.

Caterpillar Characteristics

Caterpillar short and stout, triangular in cross-section and covered in short hairs. It is bright green with yellow stripes and well camouflaged on the blackthorn it feeds on, hiding beneath the leaves by day, feeding by night.

Similar Species

Sloe and Ilex Hairstreaks have brown wings but the undersides of their wings are also brown, with red or orange spots on hind wings.

Flying Period

August–September/October.

The female Brown Hairstreaks like to lay their eggs around blackthorn bushes, while the males are seen high in the trees.

Purple Hairstreak
Quercusia quercus

24–28 mm

Adult Characteristics

Wings of males iridescent purple with black edges; of female purple-black with more or less V-shaped, iridescent purple mark at base of fore wing. Hind wings of both have small tails. Undersides grey, with dark brown and white lines near the edge and orange spots.

Habitat and Distribution

Seen flying around the tops of oak and ash trees in woodland, sometimes in large numbers; they are attracted to and feed on aphid honeydew. Found throughout much of the British Isles and Europe, north to southern Scotland and southern Scandinavia.

Caterpillar Characteristics

Caterpillar broad and flattened, reddish-brown with a dark stripe along the back and oblique stripes on the sides. It is found on oak trees, hiding in a nest of silk by day and feeding on young leaves by night.

Similar Species

Spanish Purple Hairstreaks fly around ash trees in mountains of France and Spain. They resemble Purple Hairstreaks but have wide yellow borders on the yellow-grey undersides of the wings.

Flying Period

July–September.

♂

This female Purple Hairstreak is noted for her purple-black colouring and iridescent purple mark at the base of the fore wing.

Blue-Spot Hairstreak

Strymonidia spini

28–32 mm

Adult Characteristics

Wings dark brown with small tails on hind wings and small orange spots near tails. Undersides of wings paler brown with white stripe across both wings, plus a blue spot near the tail and a row of orange spots on the hind wings.

Habitat and Distribution

Found in rough dry places from lowlands up to 1800 m, often in hills, around shrubs of blackthorn and buckthorn. Common in central and southern Europe, north to northern Germany. Absent from the northwest, including northwest France and Britain.

Caterpillar Characteristics

Caterpillar short and stout, finely hairy, green with yellow-green diagonal stripes high on its sides and a yellow stripe along its back. It feeds on blackthorn or buckthorn.

Similar Species

No other Hairstreak has a blue spot near the tail on the underside of the hind wing.

Flying Period

June–July.

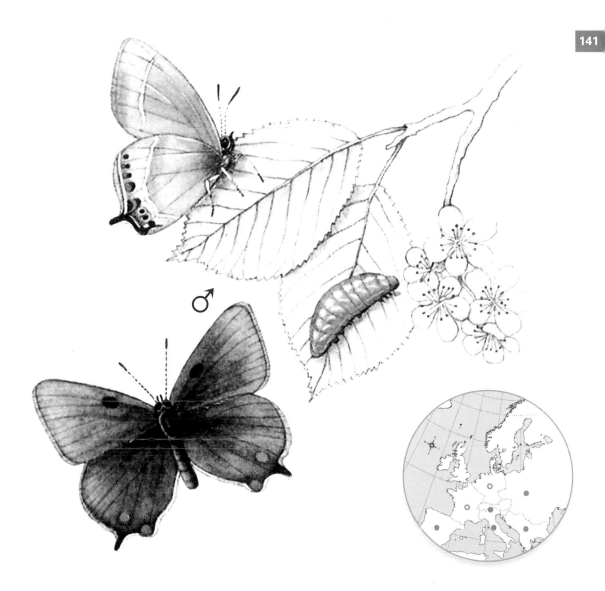

♂

White-Letter Hairstreak

Strymonidia w-album

30–32 mm

Adult Characteristics

Wings dark brown, slightly paler in females; hind wings have small tails. Undersides brown, with a white line on both wings, the line forming a 'W' near the tail of the hind wings; and a line of orange, black-centred crescents on the hind wings.

Habitat and Distribution

Rarely seen as they rest high up in elm trees in hedgerows and woods. Their numbers were drastically reduced with the death of many elms from Dutch Elm disease, but they are still found throughout much of Europe and in southern England.

Caterpillar Characteristics

Caterpillar shaped like a humped woodlouse, yellow-green with oblique white stripes on the sides and a yellow stripe along the back, camouflaged to resemble the young elm leaves on which it feeds.

Similar Species

Black Hairstreak is found locally around blackthorn across much of Europe, in the Midlands in England. Male has orange spots on rear of fore wings, female has spots on both wings.

Flying Period

June–August.

The White-Letter Hairstreak is difficult to spot as they rest high up in the trees and hedges.

Sloe Hairstreak

Nordmannia acaciae

28–32 mm

Adult Characteristics

Wings dark brown with small tails on hind wings. Undersides paler brown with white line across both wings (often faint or broken on fore wings) and orange crescents on rear of hind wings. The crescents enclose black spots near the tail.

Habitat and Distribution

Found around blackthorn bushes in rough places. Across Europe, from northern Spain eastwards to Greece and the Balkans, north to central France and southern Germany.

Caterpillar Characteristics

Caterpillar short and stout, finely hairy, yellow-green with two yellow stripes along its back. It feeds on blackthorn.

Similar Species

Ilex Hairstreak flies around oaks. It is larger, the undersides of its wings are darker and its crescents are red, with black borders. Sometimes it has an orange blotch on the fore wings.

Flying Period

June–July.

Ilex Hairstreak
Nordmannia ilicis

32–36 mm

Adult Characteristics

Wings dark brown, sometimes with an orange blotch on the fore wing. Hind wings have small tails. Undersides paler brown with irregular white line across both wings and red crescents on rear of hind wings. The crescents may have black borders with a white line on the inside.

Habitat and Distribution

Found around oaks on rough slopes from lowlands up to 1500 m in the south. Southern and central Europe, north to southern Sweden and Finland, but more common in south and scarce in north. Absent from southern Spain and Britain.

Caterpillar Characteristics

Caterpillar short and stout, light green with a black head, a black, light-edged line along its back and oblique dark stripes on the sides. It feeds on the leaves of various oak trees.

Similar Species

Sloe Hairstreak is smaller, the undersides of its wings are paler and its crescents orange; it never has an orange blotch on fore wings. It flies around blackthorn.

Flying Period

June–July.

The Ilex Hairstreak butterflies are found around oak trees throughout Europe, bar southern Spain and Britain.

Green Hairstreak

Callophrys rubi

26–30 mm

Adult Characteristics

Wings brown, with scalloped edges to hind wings. Undersides metallic green with faint or broken line of white spots across hind wings. Face of butterfly and borders around the eyes are green.

Habitat and Distribution

Found in rough ground, in woodland clearings and margins, on heaths, downs and hillsides up to 2000 m, males perching on shrubs, females around brambles, gorse and other plants. Throughout Europe and the British Isles.

Caterpillar Characteristics

Caterpillar shaped like a woodlouse, bright green with conspicuous oblique yellow stripes on the sides. It feeds on young shoots of a wide variety of plants, including gorse, broom, bird's-foot trefoil, bilberry, buckthorn and dogwood.

Similar Species

Chapman's Green Hairstreak is found only in Spain and southern France, near Strawberry Trees. It is very similar to the Green Hairstreak but has red face and red borders around eyes.

Flying Period

April–June.

The Green Hairstreak male prefers to nestle in shrubbery, whereas the females enjoy brambles and gorse.

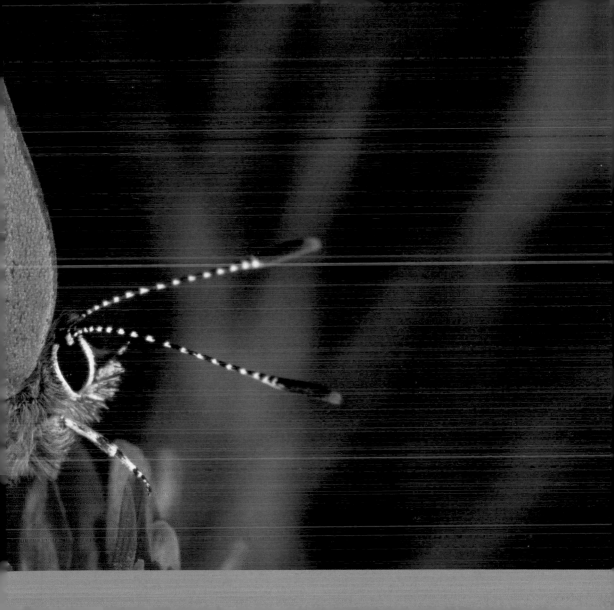

Purple-Edged Copper

32–38 mm

Palaeochrysophanus hippothoe

Adult Characteristics

Fore wings of male red-gold with black borders, often purple along the leading edge; hind wings generally darker and shot with purple. Fore wings of female generally darker with dark-brown spots and border, hind wings dark with orange marginal band.

Habitat and Distribution

Found in bogs and damp meadows, near streams and springs across much of central and northern Europe, from lowlands to 1500 m. Absent from much of northern and western France, southern Spain and Britain.

Caterpillar Characteristics

Caterpillar short and stout, deep green with short hairs, a dark line along its back and two paler lines along each side. It feeds on sorrel and bistort.

Similar Species

Violet Copper flies in wet meadows in northern Europe. Males have wings suffused with purple, females have black-marked, orange fore wings, dark-grey hind wings.

Flying Period

May–July.

Sooty Copper
Heodes tityrus

28–32 mm

Adult Characteristics

Wings of male dark grey-brown with black spots and a row of orange crescents. Fore wings of female orange with black spots and border, hind wings dark brown with an orange band on the margin enclosing black spots. Hind wings have a small lobe at the rear.

Habitat and Distribution

Found in lowland meadows and grassland across central and southern Europe, north to Germany and Poland. Absent from much of Spain (and then present in mountain meadows), northern Europe and Britain.

Caterpillar Characteristics

Caterpillar short and stout, bright green with tiny white spots, sometimes with red-brown stripes on back and sides. It may look like a small bulge in a leaf. It feeds on docks and sorrels.

Similar Species

Female **Purple-Edged Copper** similar but orange marginal band does not enclose black spots.

Scarce Copper female has orange hind wings, heavily blotched with black.

Flying Period

April–May & August–September.

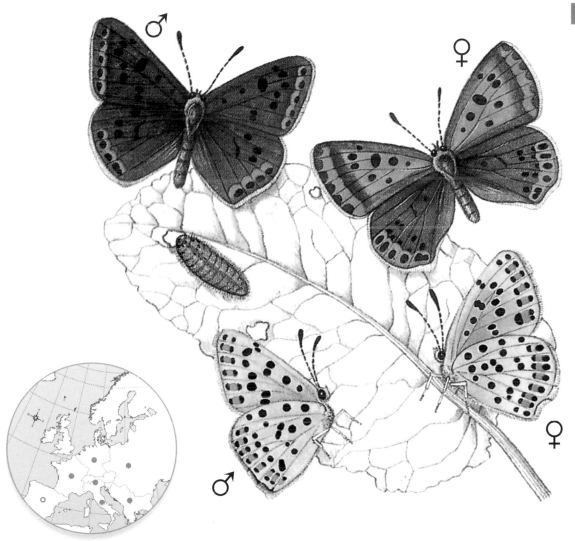

Scarce Copper

Heodes virgaureae

30–38 mm

Adult Characteristics

Wings of male brilliant copper with black borders. Wings of female also brilliant copper with many black spots. Underside of wings of both sexes yellow-red, with black spots on both wings and white spots on hind wings.

Habitat and Distribution

Found in damp meadows from lowlands to 2000 m in the south of its range. Across much of Europe from Spain to the Balkans and north to Scandinavia. Absent from lowlands of France, Belgium and the Netherlands and absent from Britain.

Caterpillar Characteristics

Caterpillar short and stout, dark green with a pale stripe along its back and each side, covered with pale hairs. It feeds on docks.

Similar Species

Purple-Shot Copper (1) flies in meadows across much of Europe but not in Britain. Male has reddish-orange wings suffused with purple, female has dark-brown wings, both with black spots.

Flying Period

July–August.

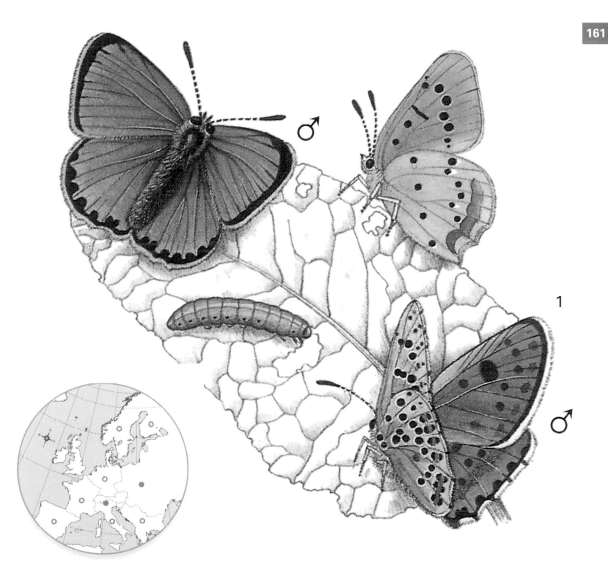

Both the male and female of the Scarce Copper species have an extraordinary vibrant orange colouring.

Large Copper
Lycaena dispar

34–40 mm

Adult Characteristics

Wings of male copper-orange with black borders and one or two black spots. Fore wings of female with many black spots, hind wings blackish with orange marginal band. Underside of fore wing orange with grey marginal band, hind wing grey with orange marginal band, both with white-ringed black spots.

Habitat and Distribution

Found locally across much of Europe, in wet meadows, marshes and fens; becoming rare due to land drainage. Became extinct in Britain in the 1850s where it lived in the eastern fenland; reintroduced to Wood Walton Fen but only surviving with help.

Caterpillar Characteristics

Caterpillar bright green with darker stripes on the side, slug-like in shape with a flattened underside. It feeds on the undersides of the leaves of water dock, chewing large holes in the leaves.

Similar Species

Scarce Copper has yellow-red undersides with black spots on both wings and white spots on hind wings.

Purple-Edged Copper females have dark fore wings as well as hind wings.

Flying Period

July–August.

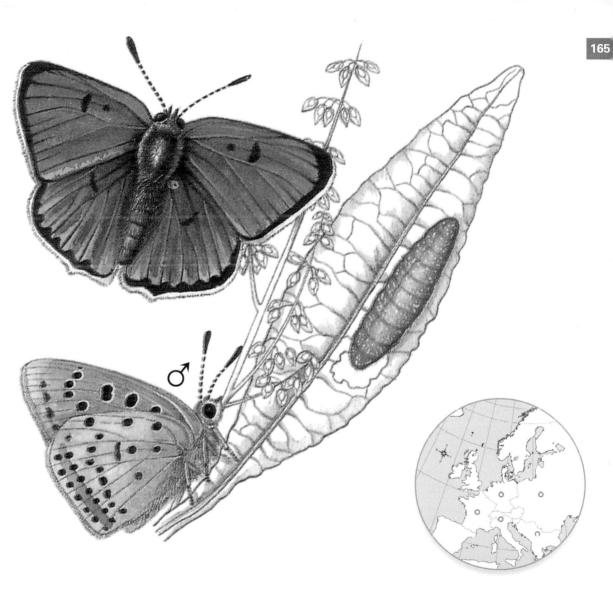

Unfortunately the Large Copper is increasingly rare across Europe, as land drainage is reducing the areas of wetland and marshes popular with this species.

Small Copper
Lycaena phlaeas

24–30 mm

Adult Characteristics

Fore wings bright orange-copper with black spots and black border; hind wings bronze-black with irregular orange stripe on rear margin. Underside of fore wing pale orange with white-ringed black spots, of hind wing pale grey with black spots and an irregular orange stripe at the rear.

Habitat and Distribution

Found in open grassland and waste places, on downs, heaths and dunes, roadside verges, anywhere its caterpillar foodplant occurs. Throughout Europe and the British Isles from lowlands to 2000 m.

Caterpillar Characteristics

Caterpillar shaped liked a dark-green woodlouse, sometimes with pink stripes. It feeds on the undersides of the leaves of sorrel and sheep's sorrel, forming characteristic grooves.

Similar Species

There are several varieties of this butterfly. One of the most common is especially frequent in Scotland and northern Europe; it has a row of blue spots on the hind wing.

Flying Period

February–October.

The grooves on the undersides of sorrel leaves indicate the caterpillar of the Small Copper, with its distinctive eating habits.

Duke of Burgundy Fritillary

Hamearis lucina

28–34 mm

Adult Characteristics

Wings dark brown with transverse rows of irregular orange spots towards the edges of the wings, larger on the fore wings and also larger in female. Underside of fore wing with similar markings, of hind wings brown with two transverse rows of white spots.

Habitat and Distribution

Found in rides and clearings in woods, in calcareous grassland and meadows, usually in lowland areas. In small local colonies across central and southern Europe from Spain to the Balkans, north to England and southern Sweden.

Caterpillar Characteristics

Caterpillar hairy, short and stout with an arched back. Pale brown, lighter on the back, with a line of dark dashes along each flank. Feeds on primroses in woodland and cowslips in grassland.

Similar Species

More closely related to blues and coppers than to other butterflies, in spite of its resemblance to a small fritillary.

Flying Period

May–June (N) & August (S).

♀

The Duke of Burgundy Fritillary butterfly lives in small colonies, particularly in France, northern Italy and westwards.

Marsh Fritillary
Eurodryas aurinia

30–46 mm

Adult Characteristics

Wings patterned in orange, yellow and dark brown with a row of black spots towards edge of hind wing. Underside of fore wings pale orange and yellow, with two orange-red patches; hind wings orange, with four pale spots near base, otherwise pattern like upper side.

Habitat and Distribution

Found in small colonies in wet grassland, moors and mountain meadows from lowlands to 1500 m. Much of the British Isles and Europe, north to southern Sweden. Absent from Norway, southern Italy and Greece.

Caterpillar Characteristics

Caterpillar black with bands of white spots on the back and sides, and with black, bristly spines. Feeds on devil's-bit scabious in Britain, on this and field scabious and plantain on the continent.

Similar Species

Most other fritillaries with similar chequered wings lack the row of black spots. Spanish Fritillary does have black spots but is confined to hills and mountains of southern Spain.

Flying Period

May–June.

The pattern on the underside of the Marsh Fritillary's wings are similar to the upper side, although the underside colouring is much paler.

Heath Fritillary

Mellicta athalia

34–46 mm

Adult Characteristics

Wings with a variable, chequered pattern of dark brown and orange, and white fringes. Underside of fore wings pale orange, yellow crescents at the margin edged with black veins. Underside of hind wings orange with two pale-yellow bands and various spots, the bands and spots edged with black.

Habitat and Distribution

Found in meadows and grassland, woodland clearings and heathland, up to 1500 m, throughout much of Europe. Formerly widespread in southern Britain but now restricted to a few colonies in Kent and the southwest.

Caterpillar Characteristics

Caterpillar black with white speckles, underside and prolegs grey-green; with fleshy orange spines and black bristles. Feeds mainly on cow-wheat and ribwort, but also on foxglove and speedwells.

Similar Species

Meadow Fritillary flies in hills and mountains of France and Spain; its orange-red wings have light, regular black markings. Provençal Fritillary is orange-yellow with light markings.

Flying Period

May–September.

The Heath Fritillary is increasingly rare in Britain and now is just found in Kent and the southwest.

False Heath Fritillary

Melitaea diamina

32–42 mm

Adult Characteristics

Wings dark brown with orange squares and spots mainly on fore wings. Underside of fore wings orange with rows of paler spots; of hind wings paler orange, with a double row of yellow and white spots in the middle, a row of yellow spots on the margin, and a row of small black and white spots between the two.

Habitat and Distribution

Found in damp lowland and mountain meadows up to 1800 m. Widespread but local from northern Spain and southern France eastwards to the Balkans and north to Scandinavia and Finland. Absent from Britain, southern Italy, southern Spain and Greece.

Caterpillar Characteristics

Caterpillar grey-brown with orange spines and a dark head. Feeds on plantains, speedwells and cow-wheats.

Similar Species

Heath Fritillary is generally less dark and lacks the row of black and white spots on the underside of the hind wing; the two species are very similar however and may be confused.

Flying Period

May–July.

Spotted Fritillary
Melitaea didyma

30–42 mm

Adult Characteristics

Wings of male tawny red with black markings varying from spots to a heavy network, but often with an unspotted band inside the black-marked borders. Of female variably flushed with grey. Underside of fore wings paler orange with yellow tips; of hind wings pale yellow with orange bands and black spots.

Habitat and Distribution

Found in woodland clearings, lowland and mountain meadows up to 1500 m throughout much of Europe, from the Mediterranean to the Baltic Sea. Absent from Britain, Holland, northern Germany, Finland and Scandinavia.

Caterpillar Characteristics

Caterpillar whitish with black lines running along the body and two rows of orange blotches along the back, each one around an orange spine; other spines whitish. Feeds on plantains, toadflax and speedwells.

Similar Species

Lesser Spotted Fritillary flies in rough grassy places in Spain and eastern Europe; it has triangular black spots on underside margin of hind wing (Spotted Fritillary spots usually round).

Flying Period

May–August.

Common to the warmer European countries, the Spotted Fritillary enjoys eating plantains, toadflax and speedwells.

Glanville Fritillary

Melitaea cinxia

28–40 mm

Adult Characteristics

Wings orange-brown with a network of black lines and veins. Underside of fore wing pale orange with dim black pattern, and yellow wing tips crossed by black lines and spots; of hind wing pale straw yellow with orange bands and rows of black spots.

Habitat and Distribution

Found in flowery meadows from lowlands to over 1800 m, throughout Europe from the south to southern Scandinavia and extreme southern Finland, but only in the Isle of Wight and Channel Islands in Britain. Absent from southern Spain.

Caterpillar Characteristics

Caterpillar black with vertical bands of white spots and short black spines on olive-green warts; head, legs and prolegs red. Feeds voraciously in groups within silken webs, usually on plantains, but also on hawkweeds and knapweeds.

Similar Species

Kanpweed Fritillary is similar but has a well-defined orange band near the edge of the hind wings without black spots; it flies in meadows and slopes in central and southern Europe.

Flying Period

May–June & August–September (S); June–July (N).

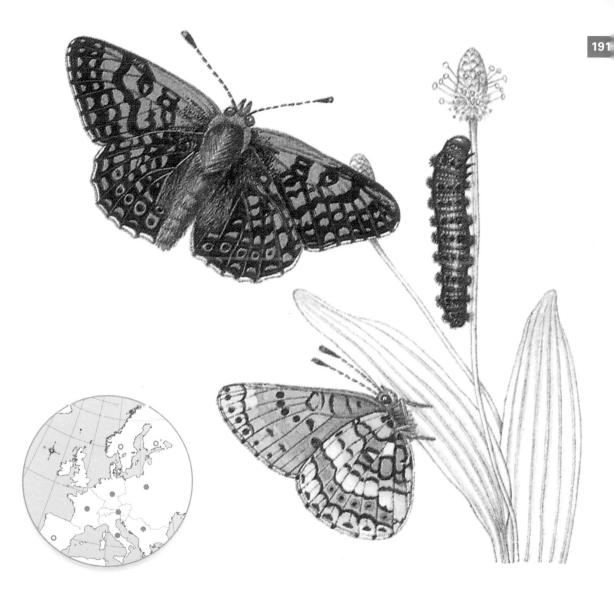

Small Pearl-Bordered Fritillary
Boloria selene

36–42 mm

Adult Characteristics

Wings bright orange-brown with many series of black spots. Underside of fore wing paler with similar pattern; of hind wing dark red-brown and yellowish, with several silver spots near the base and in the centre, and a row of black-edged silver spots around the margin.

Habitat and Distribution

Usually found in woodland clearings and margins, sometimes in meadows, marshes and open moorland, from lowlands to 1800 m. Across central Europe from Britain (but not Ireland) to Romania. Absent from southern Spain, much of Italy and Greece.

Caterpillar Characteristics

Caterpillar dark brown or black, speckled with white, with a broken white line along the back. Branched black spines have yellow bases and the two spines behind the head are longer and point forwards, like horns. Feeds on violets.

Similar Species

The very similar **Pearl-Bordered Fritillary** has different undersides to its hind wings, with one silver spot in the centre and no black edge to its marginal silver spots.

Flying Period April–May & July–August (S); June–July (N).

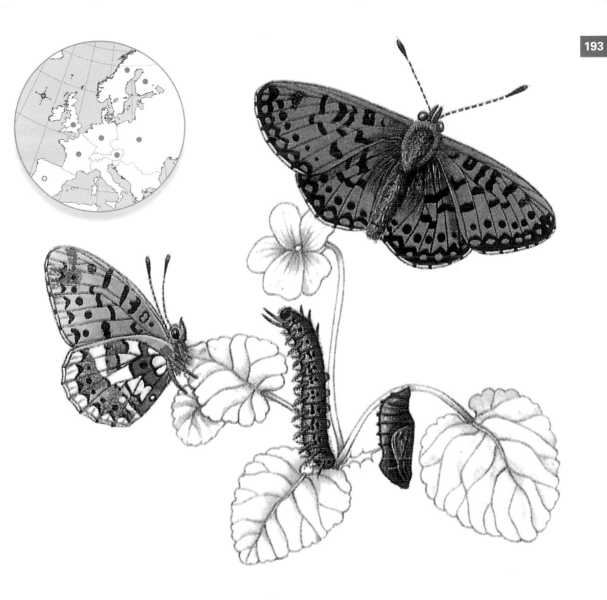

The Small Pearl-Bordered Fritillary can be seen flying from April to May and July to August in southern Europe.

Pearl-Bordered Fritillary

Boloria euphrosyne

38–46 mm

Adult Characteristics

Wings bright orange-brown with series of black spots, females larger and darker than males with heavier spots. Underside of fore wing paler with similar pattern; of hind wing pale greenish-yellow with reddish blotches, a single silver spot in the centre and a row of silver spots around the margin.

Habitat and Distribution

Found in open damp woods, meadows and heaths, from lowlands to 1800 m. Throughout much of Europe except for southern Spain. More common in the west of Britain than the east. Only in the Burren in Ireland.

Caterpillar Characteristics

Caterpillar black with a broken white line along the back and a row of white spots along each side; branched spines may be black or yellow. Feeds on violets.

Similar Species

The very similar **Small Pearl-Bordered Fritillary** has different undersides to its hind wings, with several silver spots in the centre and black-edged silver spots on the margin.

Flying Period

April–May & July–August (S); May–June (N).

The females of the Pearl-Bordered Fritillary species are larger and darker than the males, with heavier spots.

Queen of Spain Fritillary

Issoria lathonia

38–46 mm

Adult Characteristics

Fore wings concave. Wings orange-brown with rows of black spots. Underside of fore wings paler orange-brown with similar pattern of black spots; of hind wings even paler with large silver spots near base, a line of smaller, black-ringed silver spots, and another line of large silver spots around margins.

Habitat and Distribution

Found in dry open grassland, heaths and meadows from sea level to over 2000 m. Resident in southern Europe, commonly migrating north each year to reach the southern half of Scandinavia and Finland. Occasionally crossing into southern England.

Caterpillar Characteristics

Caterpillar black with bristly spines, speckled with white and with a broken yellowish stripe along each side. Feeds on violets.

Similar Species

Other fritillaries have smaller silver spots on the undersides, or lack silver spots altogether.

Flying Period

March–October.

Niobe Fritillary

Fabriciana niobe

44–60 mm

Adult Characteristics

Quite large fritillary. Wings bright orange-brown, with black spots and veins; males have two raised narrow veins on the fore wings. Underside of hind wings greenish with silver or yellowish spots; one small spot near the base of the hind wing often has a tiny black spot in its centre.

Habitat and Distribution

Found in woodland clearings, meadows and pastures, often in the mountains, up to 2500 m. Across Europe from central Spain and France to the Balkans and Greece, north to Scandinavia and Finland. Absent from Britain.

Caterpillar Characteristics

Caterpillar red-brown, mottled with black and with long pinkish, black-barbed spines. Square black spots on the back are divided by a white line running along the back and bordered by white spots. Head shaggy and yellow-brown. Feeds on violets.

Similar Species

High Brown Fritillary is generally larger; it does not have a white spot with a tiny black mark in it on the underside of the hind wing.

Flying Period

June–July.

High Brown Fritillary

Fabriciana adippe

50–62 mm

Adult Characteristics

Large fritillary. Wings bright orange-brown with black spots and veins; in males two of the veins on fore wings are raised. Underside of fore wings pale orange-brown with greenish tips, of hind wings greenish near the base, with many silver or yellowish spots and a row of reddish, silver-centred spots.

Habitat and Distribution

Found in wide woodland rides and clearings, rough grassland and heaths, especially in hills and mountains. Across the whole of Europe except for northern Scandinavia and northern Finland. Only found rarely in the southern half of Britain.

Caterpillar Characteristics

Caterpillar dark brown, variably flecked with grey, and with a white stripe along the back running through triangular dark marks. Spines pale red-brown or pink. Feeds on dog violets.

Similar Species

Niobe Fritillary is very similar. **Dark Green Fritillary** has no reddish silver-centred veins on underside of hind wing; fore wing has no raised veins.

Flying Period

June–July.

In male High Brown Fritillaries two of the veins on the fore wings are raised, helping to distinguish it from similar species.

Dark Green Fritillary

Mesoacidia aglaja

48–58 mm

Adult Characteristics

Large fritillary. Wings of male bright orange-brown with black marks and spots. Underside of fore wings pale orange-pink and of hind wings yellowish, overlaid with dull green and with large silver spots; there is a row of silver spots on the margin of both wings. Female similar but slightly paler with larger black spots.

Habitat and Distribution

Found in grassy slopes, meadows, downs, heaths and dunes, less often in grassy woodland clearings. Attracted to thistles and other purple-flowered plants. Throughout Europe and the British Isles, from lowlands high into the mountains.

Caterpillar Characteristics

Caterpillar matt black with branched black spines, white speckles and a series of orange-red blotches along each side. Feeds on violets.

Similar Species

In the **High Brown Fritillary** there is a row of reddish, silver-centred spots on the underside of each hind wing; and males have two raised veins on the fore wings.

Flying Period

June–August.

The Dark Green Fritillary is attracted to thistles and other purple-flowered plants, and interestingly the caterpillar eats violets.

Silver-Washed Fritillary

55–70 mm

Argynnis paphia

Adult Characteristics

Large fritillary. Wings of male bright orange-brown with black marks and spots; underside of fore wings tawny orange with greenish tips and similar black pattern to upper side, of hind wings greenish grey with silver stripes. Wings of female duller and paler, often with heavier black markings.

Habitat and Distribution

Found in woodland rides and clearings, often around brambles, from lowlands to 1400 m. Across Europe from Ireland and the southern half of Britain to the Balkans and Greece, north to southern Scandinavia and Finland. Absent from southern Spain.

Caterpillar Characteristics

Caterpillar has a dark-brown back with two yellow stripes, mottled brown sides with darker lines, and black-tipped, red-brown spines; the first two spines are black and point forwards over the head. Feeds on violets.

Similar Species

The **Cardinal** is similar but its fore wing undersides are rosy red at the base, green at the tips, and its hind wing undersides are light green with silver streaks.

Flying Period End of June–August.

The Silver-Washed Fritillary is a large species; the male is particularly striking and the female is paler and often has heavier, darker markings.

Other Fritillaries

♀

Cardinal

Wingspan: 64–80 mm. The largest European fritillary. Wings orange-brown with black spots and marks. Male somewhat, female more heavily flushed with green-grey. Female larger. Underside of fore wings rose-red at base, green at tips; of hind wing green, with narrow silver stripes more obvious in female. Found in woods and meadows to 2000 m, across southern Europe from Spain and southern France to the Balkans and Greece. Flies June–July. Caterpillar feeds on violets.

Other Fritillaries

♂

Lesser Marbled Fritillary

Wingspan: 34–40 mm. Wings orange-red with linear black markings and black borders. Flies in wet marshy meadows up to 1500 m in central and northern Europe, in June–July. Caterpillar feeds on meadowsweet, burnet and related plants. Marbled Fritillary is similar but larger (wingspan 42–52 mm), with orange-red wings and black spots and marks. It flies in June–July in warm valleys in southern and eastern Europe. Caterpillar feeds on brambles and violets.

Other Fritillaries

Cranberry Fritillary

Wingspan: 32–42 mm. Wings bright tawny-red with V-shaped black marks in the middle of the fore wing, and other distinct zig-zagging marks and spots on both wings. Found in peat-bogs from lowlands to mountains, in northern Europe. Flies June–July. Caterpillar feeds on cranberry. The similar Shepherd's Fritillary flies high in the mountains of central and southern Europe. It has less definite, less zig-zagging markings.

Other Fritillaries

Scarce Fritillary

Wingspan: 42–50 mm. Wings banded and spotted in dark brown, orange-red and pale yellow; with two large, black-edged orange-red spots near top middle of fore wing, separated by a yellow space, and a series of small white spots on hind wings. Found locally, often in valleys or near streams, scattered across Europe, east, northeast and southeast of Paris. Flies May–June. Caterpillars hibernate in silken webs on trees, then disperse to feed on plantains, speedwells and other plants.

Other Fritillaries

Bog Fritillary

Wingspan: 40–46 mm. Wings tawny-yellow with dark zig-zag markings and spots. Underside of hind wing yellow and orange, with bands of large, gleaming yellow or white spots in the middle and on the margin, and a row of black-edged, small white spots near the edge. Found in marshes, wet meadows and bogs, scattered very locally in northern and central Europe. Flies June–July. Caterpillar feeds on bistort, violets and cranberry.

Other Fritillaries

Violet Fritillary

Wingspan: 32–34 mm. Wings tawny-orange with clear black marks and spots. Underside of hind wing suffused with purple, with a band of clear white spots across the middle, and a row of prominent black, white-centred spots towards the margin. Found in open woods, heathland and hills up to 900 m, all across central Europe from France and Belgium eastward, and north to Scandinavia. Flies April–September. Caterpillar feeds on violets and brambles.

Unfortunately, the numbers of Violet Fritillaries are in decline due to the eradication of their preferred habitat – uncultivated meadows.

European Map

Araschnia levana

30–38 mm

Adult Characteristics

Spring form has red-brown wings with black marks and spots; undersides also red-brown with white veins and cross-lines, and a broad, broken white band, often across both wings. Late summer form black with a broken, white or pale-yellow band across both wings; underside similar to spring form.

Habitat and Distribution

Found in woodland rides and clearings, around woodland margins and riversides. Mainly in lowland areas across central Europe from western France eastwards to Romania, and in northern Spain. Absent from the south and north, and from Britain.

Caterpillar Characteristics

Caterpillar black with white speckles, yellow or black spines and yellow prolegs. Feeds in groups on stinging nettles.

Similar Species

Spring form is like a small fritillary. Late summer form is like a small **White Admiral.**

Flying Period

April–June & August–September.

European Maps vary in colour. The spring brood have red-brown wings with black marks, whereas the summer brood have black wings with a pale band.

Painted Lady

Cynthia cardui

54–58 mm

Adult Characteristics

Wings tawny-orange to pinkish buff, with black, white-spotted tips to fore wings, and rows of black spots on hind wings. One blue spot occurs at inside rear edge of hind wing. Underside of fore wing pink and black with white spots; hind wing variegated in pale browns, black and white, with a row of eye-spots.

Habitat and Distribution

Resident in Africa, migrating north each year to reach almost all Europe, commonly in Britain and southern Scandinavia. Found in many habitats, often in open countryside or waste land, attracted by flowers. Does not overwinter in Europe.

Caterpillar Characteristics

Caterpillar black, speckled with tiny white spots and with many black or yellowish spines; it has a discontinuous yellow line along each side. Feeds mainly on thistles, also on nettles or mallows, forming silken webs on the underside of the leaves.

Similar Species

Tortoiseshells do not have black, white-spotted wing tips, their wings lack the pinkish tinge and they have a row of blue spots on their hind wings.

Flying Period

April–October (N); most of year (S).

Arguably an adventurous species, the Painted Lady migrates from Africa each year and travels as far north as Scandinavia.

Peacock

Inachis io

54–60 mm

Adult Characteristics

Wings brownish-red with a single large 'peacock' eyespot, ringed with yellow and black, on each wing. Underside almost black, metallic, crossed by fine dark lines.

Habitat and Distribution

Mobile butterflies found in many habitats, rural and urban, attracted by flowers. Widespread and often common throughout much of Europe and Britain, becoming more rare in Scotland and absent from northern Scandinavia and much of Finland.

Caterpillar Characteristics

Caterpillar velvety black, covered with black spines, speckled with white spots. Prolegs yellow-brown. Feeds on stinging nettles, at first in groups in silken webs, later leaving the webs and dispersing.

Similar Species

No similar butterfly.

Flying Period

February–May & July–September.

The Peacock is a common European butterfly and can be distinguished by the 'peacock' eyespots on its wings, from which it takes its name.

Comma
Polygonia c-album

44–48 mm

Adult Characteristics

Wings tawny orange with dark markings and irregular, scalloped margins. Undersides variegated dark brown and yellow brown, with a silver 'comma' mark on the hind wing. Some individuals in the summer have less deeply scalloped wing margins and brighter, paler wings, with paler undersides.

Habitat and Distribution

Found in open countryside, in gardens, around woodland margins from lowlands to 1800 m throughout much of Europe, north to Sweden, Finland, the southern half of England and Wales. Also migrating into Norway.

Caterpillar Characteristics

Caterpillar black with orange-brown bands on its sides and a large white patch on its back; it resembles a bird dropping. Spines light orange-brown, but white on white patch. Feeds singly on the undersides of stinging-nettle leaves.

Similar Species

Southern Comma is found in hot dry places across southern Europe; it has yellow-brown wings with small black spots and a small 'Y' mark on the underside of the hind wing.

Flying Period

March–April & June–August.

The Comma displays beautiful scalloped wings and tawny-orange markings.

Small Tortoiseshell

Aglais urticae

44–50 mm

Adult Characteristics

Wings orange-red, darker towards base; large black blotches on fore wings separated by pale yellow spaces with a white space towards the tip. There are blue crescents around margins of both wings. Underside dark grey near base and yellow-brown towards margins, markings similar to those on upper surface.

Habitat and Distribution

Highly mobile, migrant butterflies which may be seen in any habitat, rural or urban, attracted by flowers. Common throughout Europe and Britain from sea level to over 2000 m.

Caterpillar Characteristics

Caterpillar has many spines; it has a black back with tiny white spots, two discontinuous yellow bands along the sides, and may be black or yellow on the underside. Feeds on stinging nettles, at first in groups in silken webs, later singly.

Similar Species

Large Tortoiseshell is larger, with darker yellow spaces between the black marks on the fore wings, with no white space near the fore-wing tip.

Flying Period

March–October.

The Small Tortoiseshell is attracted to flowers regardless of whether they are at sea level or at an altitude of over 2000 m.

Large Tortoiseshell
Nymphalis polychloros

50–62 mm

Adult Characteristics

Wings with ragged margins, orange-brown with several black blotches on fore wings separated by yellow spaces; black marginal borders enclose orange-brown and blue crescents (blue ones usually only on hind wings). Underside dark brown near base, paler and yellow-brown towards edges. Legs dark brown.

Habitat and Distribution

Found in open woods and around woodland margins throughout much of continental Europe, migrating into Scandinavia and southern Finland each year. In Britain it is found mainly in southern England and is absent from Ireland.

Caterpillar Characteristics

Caterpillar black with white speckles, orange lines along back and sides, and many sharp, forked, yellowish spines. Feeds in groups, on leaves of elms and willows, at first in conspicuous silken webs, later leaving the webs but staying in groups.

Similar Species

Scarce Tortoiseshell is similar but has pale brown or buff legs; it flies in woods in eastern Europe.

Small Tortoiseshell has white, not yellow, space near tip of fore wings.

Flying Period

June–September & April–May.

Despite migrating as far north as Finland each year, the Large Tortoiseshell does not travel to Ireland and in Britain it remains mainly in the southern counties.

Camberwell Beauty

Nymphalis antiopa

60–65 mm

Adult Characteristics

Wings dark purple-brown with a row of bright blue spots near the edges and ragged yellow margins. Underside mottled grey with a yellowish border.

Habitat and Distribution

Found in light woodland and open countryside, often in hills and mountains. Scattered throughout much of continental Europe, migrating into Scandinavia and Finland each year but a rare migrant in Britain. Absent from most of Spain except the north.

Caterpillar Characteristics

Caterpillar black with many tiny white spots and red blotches along its sides; it has many black spines and bristles. Feeds in groups in a silken web at first, later in groups or alone, on willows, birch and elm.

Similar Species

No similar butterfly.

Flying Period

Spring–late autumn.

Red Admiral
Vanessa atalanta

56–62 mm

Adult Characteristics

Wings black with red stripe across fore wings and along rear of hind wings (containing black spots on hind wings), white spots on fore wing tips and a broken white line around both wings. Underside of fore wing blackish, brown and white on tips with a red bar across; of hind wings mottled brown, black and blue.

Habitat and Distribution

Found in many urban and rural habitats; attracted to flowers, and to fallen fruits in late summer. Most of Europe but only overwintering south of the Alps, migrating north in large numbers each year, to northern Britain and Scandinavia.

Caterpillar Characteristics

Caterpillar usually black with yellow spots along the sides and black spines; less often grey-green or yellowish with pale spines. Feeds on stinging nettles, singly at first in silken webs, later within curled leaves.

Similar Species

No other European butterfly is quite like this one.

Flying Period

May–October.

In late summer the Red Admiral can be found near flowers and the fallen fruits of the season all over Europe.

White Admiral

Limenitis camilla

52–60 mm

Adult Characteristics

Wings brown-black with a wide band of white spots, and other white spots towards the tip of the fore wing; and with three rows of black spots towards the edges of both wings. Underside tawny orange, grey near inner edge of hind wings, and with similar markings to upper side.

Habitat and Distribution

Found in rides and clearings in damp woods from lowlands to 900 m. Across central Europe from northern Spain, France and southern Britain to Romania and north to southern Sweden. Absent from southeastern France, southern Italy and Greece.

Caterpillar Characteristics

Caterpillar green with a purplish underside and two rows of brown spines along its back. Feeds on honeysuckle.

Similar Species

Southern White Admiral has blue-edged dark spots near wing margins; found in woods in southern Europe.

Common Glider has three bands of white spots; found in woods in eastern Europe.

Flying Period

June–July.

The markings on the White Admiral's wings are largely symmetrical.

Poplar Admiral
Limenitis populi

70–80 mm

Adult Characteristics

Wings dark brown with bands of white spots, often indistinct in male, larger and better defined in female, and orange and black spots around the margins, larger on hind wings. Underside orange with similar markings in blue-grey or white and a double row of black spots near the edges of the hind wings.

Habitat and Distribution

Found in damp open woods and forests, usually among the tree tops. From sea level to 1000 m, from southeastern France eastwards, migrating to Scandinavia and Finland some years. Absent from western France, Spain, Portugal and Britain.

Caterpillar Characteristics

Caterpillar green with a yellowish band along its sides, and purple-brown spots along its back and beneath the band. It has two rows of spiny projections along its back, the first two long and pointing forward. Feeds on aspen and other poplars.

Similar Species

White Admiral has much darker wings and no orange spots around the margin.

Purple Emperors have wings flushed with purple and one or more solitary dark spots.

Flying Period

June–July.

Purple Emperor
Apatura iris

62–74 mm

Adult Characteristics

Wings of male almost black flushed with iridescent purple; three interrupted lines of white spots on fore wing, one on hind wing with a single dark spot. Female paler with no purple sheen and broader creamy white spots. Undersides brown and grey with similar markings plus an extra dark spot on fore wing.

Habitat and Distribution

Found in old deciduous woodland and around old hedgerows. Mainly in lowlands, across central Europe from northern Spain and southern Britain eastward; absent from much of southern Europe (including south of France and Italy), and Scandinavia.

Caterpillar Characteristics

Caterpillar shaped like a woodlouse with a pointed tail. It is green and granular in appearance with diagonal yellow lines; its head has two pink-tipped, forward-pointed horns. Feeds on leaves of goat willow, grey and crack willows.

Similar Species

Lesser Purple Emperor has dark, orange-ringed spots on the fore wings. **Admirals** have bands of white spots but no single dark spots and their wings are not flushed with purple.

Flying Period

July–August.

The male Purple Emperor has a glorious purple gleam to his wings, whereas the female has no purple sheen and is paler, with large creamy spots.

Lesser Purple Emperor
Apatura ilia

64–70 mm

Adult Characteristics

Similar to Purple Emperor but with a large, dark, orange-ringed spot on each fore wing. Underside may be suffused with brown all over.

Habitat and Distribution

Found in woodland, often in damp places or near streams, across central Europe from France to Romania, north to Poland in the east. Absent from northwest including Britain, Holland and northwest Germany. Also absent from southern Italy and Greece.

Caterpillar Characteristics

Caterpillar shaped like woodlouse, tapering towards the pointed tail. It is green with diagonal red and yellow stripes and with two long forward-pointing, brown-tipped horns on its head. Feeds on poplar, aspen and willows.

Similar Species

Purple Emperor lacks the dark, orange-ringed spots on the fore wings. **Admirals** have no single ringed spots and their wings are not flushed with purple.

Flying Period

May–June & August–September.

The orange spot on the fore wing and the often brown underside of the Lesser Purple Emperor help to distinguish it from the Purple Emperor.

Two-Tailed Pasha

Charaxes jasius

76–82 mm

Adult Characteristics

Wings rich brown with wide yellow-brown margins, the hind wings with black borders outside the yellow margins and blue spots inside, also with two tails. Underside brown with white-ringed dark spots and bands of white and yellow towards the edges.

Habitat and Distribution

Found locally in dry hills up to 800 m, around the Mediterranean coastline from France to Greece. Absent from Spain and Portugal and from the Adriatic coast.

Caterpillar Characteristics

Caterpillar green and covered with many tiny white dots; it has two dark-ringed, blue-centred yellow spots on its back and a large head with four backward-pointing prongs tipped with red. Feeds on leaves of strawberry trees.

Similar Species

No similar species.

Flying Period

May–June & August–September.

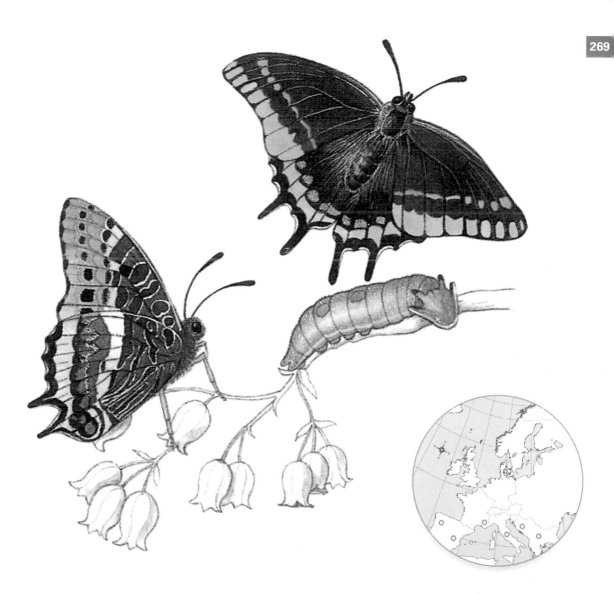

Marbled White

Melanargia galathea

46–56 mm

Adult Characteristics

Wings of male black with creamy white markings, consisting of an irregular band of blotches across the centre of both wings, with spots on either side. Underside with similar pattern but black areas flushed with white. Female similar but markings larger and whiter; underside of hind wing flushed with yellow.

Habitat and Distribution

Found in grassland and on downs, also on roadside verges and around woodland margins, from sea level to 1500 m. Throughout much of Europe from the Mediterranean to the Baltic coast, also in southern England and Wales. Absent from Scandinavia.

Caterpillar Characteristics

Caterpillar spindle-shaped, tapering at the tail to two reddish points; either light brown or yellow-green with darker and paler stripes along back and sides. Feeds on grasses, probably mainly fescues.

Similar Species

Several other Marbled Whites fly in southern Europe, three in Spain. In general their wings have much more extensive white markings, with the black areas much reduced and more delicate.

Flying Period

June–July.

The males and females of the Marbled White have a similar appearance, although the female has larger whiter markings.

Great Banded Grayling

Brintesia circe

66–80 mm

Adult Characteristics

Wings black with a wide broken band of white across both wings and a single black spot on fore wing. Hind wings have scalloped margins. Underside similar in pattern but dark area mottled.

Habitat and Distribution

Found in open deciduous woodland, especially oak woods, often sitting on tree trunks, from lowlands to about 1400 m. Across southern and central Europe from Portugal and France east to Czechoslovakia and Greece.

Caterpillar Characteristics

Caterpillar tapering from its striped head to the two points on its tail; it is very light brown on the back and sides, with dark-brown stripes and a yellow-brown stripe on each side, and dark brown beneath. Feeds on brome and rye grasses.

Similar Species

No similar species.

Flying Period

June–July.

The scalloped hind wings and wide band of broken white colouring mark the Great Banded Grayling.

Woodland Grayling
Hipparchia fagi

66–76 mm

Adult Characteristics

Wings dark grey-brown, with broad yellow-white bands near margins and two eye-spots on fore wing, one on hind wing; band and spots more distinct in female. Hind wings have scalloped margins. Underside of fore wing has similar pattern, hind wing banded in mottled grey and white.

Habitat and Distribution

Found in open woods and woodland margins, often resting on tree trunks with wings open; from lowlands to 1000 m. Scattered locally across central and southern Europe, from northern Spain and southern France to southern Poland and Greece.

Caterpillar Characteristics

Caterpillar tapering from head to two points at the tail; pale brown in colour with darker brown lines along back and sides. Feeds on soft grasses, particularly on bromes and fescues.

Similar Species

Rock Grayling (1) is similar but smaller (wingspan 56–66 mm); it is found from Spain across central Europe but generally flies in the mountains, in rough places up to 1500 m or more.

Flying Period

July–August.

1

Grayling
Hipparchia semele

42–50 mm

Adult Characteristics

Wings brown with variable yellowish bands near margins (larger in female), containing two white-centred, black spots on fore wing, one on hind wing. Hind wings scalloped on margins. Underside of fore wing tawny orange and brown, hind wing marbled brown, grey and black, both with spots as upper side.

Habitat and Distribution

Found in sheltered sunny places, in heaths and rough hillsides, coastal cliffs and dunes, dry woods and downs, from lowlands to 1500 m. Throughout Europe north to southern Scandinavia and Finland. Mostly around the coasts in Britain and Ireland.

Caterpillar Characteristics

Caterpillar cigar-shaped, tapering to two points at the tail; head and body pale yellow-brown with darker brown stripes. Feeds on grasses by night, hiding by day.

Similar Species

Southern Grayling is almost indistinguishable but only found in Mediterranean islands and Greece.

False Grayling has only one black spot on the fore wing, Baltic Grayling has several.

Flying Period

May–August.

Sheltered heaths, hillsides, cliffs and dunes, as well as woodland, are favoured by the Grayling.

Tree Grayling
Neohipparchia statilinus

44–46 mm

Adult Characteristics

Wings dark grey-brown, paler towards margin with two black and two white spots on fore wing, one black spot on hind wing. In female black spots usually white-centred. Underside of fore wing similar to upper side, hind wing mottled in browns with sinuous black line across middle. Hind wing has scalloped edge.

Habitat and Distribution

Found in open woodland, scrub and heathland, often in hills. Scattered across central and southern Europe, from Portugal and France to Poland, becoming rare in many places.

Caterpillar Characteristics

Caterpillar tapers from head to the two points on the tail; it is pale brown in colour with darker brown lines along back and sides. Feeds on grasses, especially barren brome.

Similar Species

Striped Grayling has similar upper surface, but its hind wing underside has striking zig-zag pattern of dark lines; it flies in rocky places along trees in southern France and Iberia.

Flying Period

July–September.

False Grayling

Arethusana arethusa

44–48 mm

Adult Characteristics

Wings brown with a variable orange band across both wings and a single dark spot on both wings. Underside of fore wing mostly orange with a single dark spot, of hind wing mottled dark brown with white band towards margin. Hind wings have scalloped margins. Female larger than male, with wider orange bands.

Habitat and Distribution

Found in heaths and grassy limestone places, up to 1200 m. Widely distributed but local in southern Europe, from Portugal and France to eastern Europe and the Balkans.

Caterpillar Characteristics

Caterpillar tapering from its striped head to the two points on its tail; it is yellow-brown or grey, with dark-brown stripes. Feeds on grasses, particularly on fescues.

Similar Species

Baltic Grayling has dark-brown wings with a band of orange patches on both wings, some with black spots. It is one of several northern graylings found in Scandinavia and Finland.

Flying Period

July–August.

The single dark spot on the fore wing, containing a white dot helps to distinguish the False Grayling from the similar looking Grayling.

Ringlet
Aphantopus hyperantus

40–48 mm

Adult Characteristics

Wings dark brown to almost black, female paler than male; male with or without, and female with, more or less dim eyespots on both wings. Undersides of both sexes paler and may be flushed with gold, with two conspicuous white-centred, yellow-ringed eyespots on each fore wing, five on hind wing.

Habitat and Distribution

Found in damp meadows, open woods, hedges and woodland margins, from lowlands to 1500 m. Most of Europe and the British Isles, from northern Spain to southern Scotland, southern Scandinavia and Finland. Absent from southern Italy and most of Greece.

Caterpillar Characteristics

Caterpillar tapering towards the two points of the tail; yellowish and covered with dark bristles, with a white line along the back and several dark lines along the sides. Feeds on grasses, especially on tufted hair-grass or creeping bent.

Similar Species

False Ringlet is smaller, with underside eyespots on hind wing arranged four and one (not three and two as in Ringlet); it flies in wet meadows in parts of southern-central Europe.

Flying Period

June–August.

The female Ringlet has eyespots on both wings, but males do not always have the same marking.

Woodland Ringlet

Erebia medusa

38–50 mm

Adult Characteristics

Wings of male dark brown, generally with two or three large and two small eyespots on fore wing, four on hind wing, all with orange-yellow circles around. Underside paler, uniform brown with similar eyespots. Female larger and paler, orange-yellow circles more extensive and more or less touching.

Habitat and Distribution

Found in damp meadows, moors and damp woods in lowlands in the north of its range, in damp mountain meadows in the south. From central France and Germany east to Poland, southeast to Greece. Absent from Spain, the Pyrenees and southwest Alps.

Caterpillar Characteristics

Caterpillar tapering from head to the two points at the tail, green or brown with a black band along the back and pale stripes along the sides. Feeds on grasses, especially crab grass and wood millet.

Similar Species

One of many ringlets in Europe, most mountain species. Mountain Ringlet flies in southern Europe, Scotland and the Lake District; it is brown with red bands and black spots.

Flying Period

May–July.

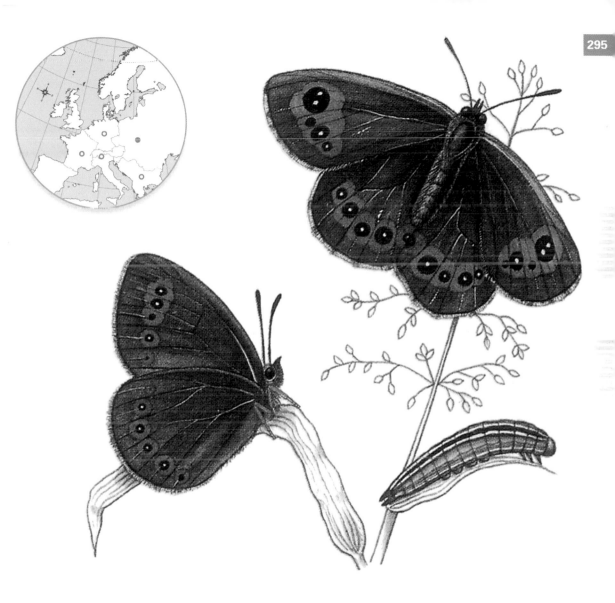

The Woodland Ringlet is not widespread in Europe. It is most frequently found in central eastern Europe.

Arran Brown

Erebia ligea

48–54 mm

Adult Characteristics

Wings of male black with wide red band on both wings, three or four white-centred eyespots on fore wing, three on hind wing. Underside of fore wing similar to upper side of hind wing, banded in light and dark brown, with an irregular white streak. Female similar but dark brown with orange-red band.

Habitat and Distribution

Found in meadows and woods in hilly country, up to 1500 m, through the Alps and Carpathians to the Balkans and Greece. Also in lowland areas of Scandinavia and Finland. Reported in Arran and the Scottish Highlands.

Caterpillar Characteristics

Caterpillar tapering from its head to the two points on its tail, pale brown or yellowish with a dark line running down its back and a broad white stripe on each side. Takes two years before it pupates. Feeds on crab grass and wood millet.

Similar Species

Scotch Argus (1) flies in meadows and woods, in hills of central Europe, Scotland and Cumbria. Male black, female dark brown, both with red bands and three eyespots on each wing.

Flying Period

July–August.

1

The Arran Brown is found in hilly country, up to 1500 m, and has been sighted in the Scottish Highlands.

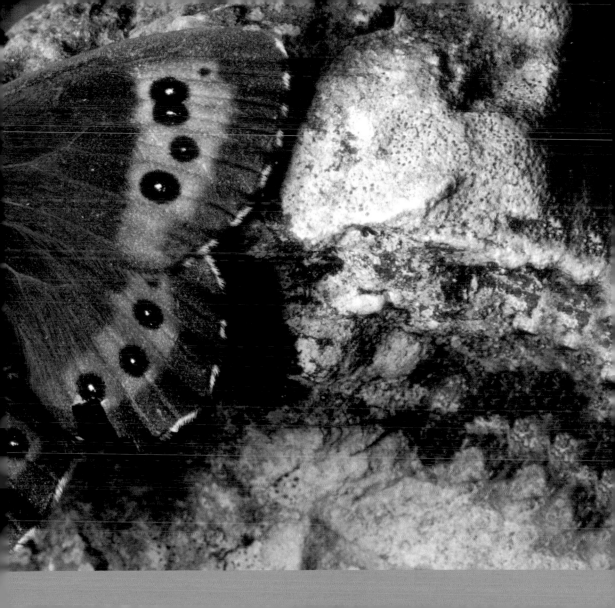

Meadow Brown

Maniola jurtina

40–58 mm

Adult Characteristics

Wings of male dark brown with white-centred eyespot on fore wing. Underside of fore wing flushed with orange; of hind wing dark at base, paler and yellower towards margin with two small black spots. Female paler with orange area on both wings; underside of fore wing orange, hind wing often brightly banded.

Habitat and Distribution

Found in grassy places, meadows, roadside verges, grassy woodland rides and clearings, from sea level to about 1800 m. Throughout the British Isles and much of Europe, north to southern Scandinavia and Finland.

Caterpillar Characteristics

Caterpillar tapering from head towards the two white points of the tail; yellow-green on the back and darker green beneath, with a white line along each side and covered with long whitish hairs. Feeds on grasses, especially meadow grasses.

Similar Species

A very variable species. Males may have a flush of orange beneath the eyespot on fore wings. Particularly brightly coloured males are found in western Scotland.

Flying Period

June–September.

The particularly brightly coloured male Meadow Browns are found in western Scotland.

Dusky Meadow Brown

Hyponephele lycaon

40–48 mm

Adult Characteristics

Fore wings grey-brown, males slightly flushed with orange, a narrow dark streak across the middle and a single black spot; females heavily flushed with orange and two black spots. Hind wings of both grey-brown with a scalloped margin. Undersides similar but with more orange and black spots white-centred.

Habitat and Distribution

Found in dry rocky places, mainly in lowland areas. Central and southern Europe from the Mediterranean to Finland, but absent from most of France, the Netherlands, Scandinavia and Britain.

Caterpillar Characteristics

Caterpillar tapering towards the two points of the tail. It is bright green with two stripes on each side in differing shades of yellow. Its head is green with a white-edged black stripe at the back. Feeds on grasses, especially meadow grasses.

Similar Species

The one black spot on the fore wing of the **Meadow Brown** is white-centred on both sides of the wing.

Flying Period

July–August.

Large Heath
Coenonympha tullia

30–44 mm

Adult Characteristics

Wings of male mid to dark brown, female light to mid brown, both with yellow-ringed spots on both wings. Underside of both sexes variably banded, grey near the margin and dark brown near the base with an irregular white streak across the centre; fore wing has single eyespot and hind wing has row of eyespots.

Habitat and Distribution

Found in marshes and wet meadows, peat bogs and rough wet moorlands, often among cotton grass, from lowlands to 600 m. Central and northern Europe, from France eastward and north across much of Scandinavia; northern half of the British Isles.

Caterpillar Characteristics

Caterpillar tapering towards the two pink points of the tail; green with a dark line along the back and several yellow or white lines along the sides. Feeds on white beak-sedge and probably on cotton grass.

Similar Species

A common northern form is yellow-brown flushed with grey, and often lacks eyespots. **Chestnut Heath** (1) flies in grassy places, locally across Europe from northern Spain to Finland.

Flying Period

June–July.

1

Both male and female Large Heaths have yellow-ringed spots on both wings, however the northern form often lack eyespots.

Small Heath
Coenonympha pamphilus

26–34 mm

Adult Characteristics

Wings bright yellow-brown with narrow grey borders and a small grey spot on each fore wing. Underside of fore wing orange near base, paler towards margin with a large, yellow-ringed eyespot; of hind wing olive-brown near base, a pale band across the centre, and grey towards margin with several eyespots.

Habitat and Distribution

Found in grassy places from sea level to 1800 m. Common throughout the British Isles and Europe except the far north of Scandinavia.

Caterpillar Characteristics

Caterpillar tapers towards the two pink points of the tail; it is green with whitish green lines along the body. Feeds on various grasses, including meadow grasses and fescues.

Similar Species

Large Heath is larger and has no grey wing borders.

Flying Period

May–September.

The Small Heath is distinguishable from the Large Heath not only by its small size, but also by the narrow grey borders on its wings.

Pearly Heath
Coenonympha arcania

34–40 mm

Adult Characteristics

Fore wing orange with wide dark border; hind wing dark with a trace of orange at rear, often with one or two eyespots. Underside orange-brown, with a metallic border on hind wing, sometimes on fore wing; hind wing crossed by an irregular pale band and with several yellow-ringed, white-centred eyespots.

Habitat and Distribution

Found in open grassy woodland and around grassy slopes, often in hills, from lowlands to 1200 m. Northern Portugal and Spain across Europe to Poland, southern Scandinavia and Greece. Absent from Britain.

Caterpillar Characteristics

Caterpillar tapering to the two red-marked points of its tail; green with a dark line along its back and yellow lines along each side. Feeds on grasses, especially on melick.

Similar Species

Darwin's Heath and Alpine Heath are similar but smaller; they are found only in high alpine meadows in the Alps and Dolomites.

Flying Period

June–July.

Gatekeeper
Pyronia tithonus

34–38 mm

Adult Characteristics

Wings dark brown, with large orange patch on fore wing, smaller one on hind wing; and a single eyespot on each wing, the one on fore wing larger and with two white spots. Female has larger, brighter patches than male. Underside of hind wing (in both sexes) banded in brown and yellow, with small eyespots.

Habitat and Distribution

Found around brambles in hedgerows, woodland clearings and lanes, in lowland areas throughout much of Europe, north to Germany and Poland. Absent from Scandinavia and southern Italy. Also found in England, Wales and the far south of Ireland.

Caterpillar Characteristics

Caterpillar tapering towards the two points of the tail, yellow-white with darker speckles and many short whitish hairs; there is a dark line along the back and paler lines along the sides. Feeds on a variety of grasses, often on fescues and bents.

Similar Species

Southern Gatekeeper has no eyespots on underside of hind wing and male has dark markings on fore wing. It flies in hot dry bushy places from Portugal across southern Europe to Greece.

Flying Period

July–August.

The female Gatekeeper has larger, brighter orange patches than the male.

Wall Brown

Lasiommata megera

36–50 mm

Adult Characteristics

Fore wing orange-brown with brown borders, a network of brown veins and an eyespot; hind wing brown with orange patches and white-centred eyespots. Underside of fore wing similar to but paler than upper side; of hind wing banded and mottled in browns with a row of brown, black-centred eyespots.

Habitat and Distribution

Found in dry open grassland, roadsides and waste places, gardens and fields, heaths and cliffs, woodland clearings and hedgerows, from sea level to 1500 m. Throughout Europe, north to southern Scandinavia. Also in England, Wales and Ireland.

Caterpillar Characteristics

Caterpillar tapering towards the two points of the tail; blue-green, covered with whitish hairs, and with yellow-white lines along back and sides. Feeds on a variety of grasses.

Similar Species

Large Wall Brown and Northern Wall Brown have much less orange on their wings, and although they have dark veins, their wings do not appear to be latticed.

Flying Period

March–September.

The large areas of orange colour on the Wall Brown's wings distinguish it from the less vibrant Large Wall Brown.

Large Wall Brown
Lasiommata maera

44–56 mm

Adult Characteristics

Fore wings brown with dark veins and a white-centred black eyespot (sometimes with two white spots) in an orange patch; hind wing with two or three white-centred eyespots in orange rings. Underside of fore wing similar but brighter, of hind wing mottled brown with a row of brown-ringed eyespots.

Habitat and Distribution

Found in rocky places, woodland clearings and margins, often on hillside slopes, from lowlands to mountains, up to 1800 m. Common throughout most of Europe, but absent from Britain and parts of northern Scandinavia.

Caterpillar Characteristics

Caterpillar tapering towards the two points of the tail; pale green with a dark-brown back stripe, two yellow stripes on each side, and a dark-green stripe beneath the lower yellow one. Feeds on grasses, including wood barley and meadow grasses.

Similar Species

Northern Wall Brown is smaller, with dark cross-lines on fore wing and a wavy transverse line on hind wing. It flies in coniferous woods in southern Europe, Scandinavia and Finland.

Flying Period

May–June & August–September (S); June–July (N).

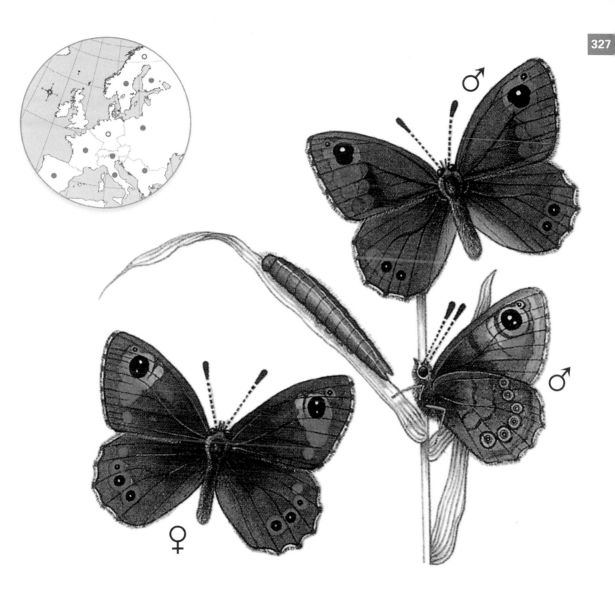

Speckled Wood

Pararge aegeria

38–44 mm

Adult Characteristics

Wings grey-brown with pale yellow or orange patches, more on fore wings; one eyespot on fore wing, three on hind wing in orange or yellow patches. Underside of fore wing patterned in orange and brown or yellow and brown; of hind wing banded in shades of yellow-brown, tinged with green and with white spots.

Habitat and Distribution

Found in dappled sunlight and shade, in open woods, woodland rides and clearings. Throughout Europe north to central Scandinavia and Finland.

Caterpillar Characteristics

Caterpillar tapering towards the two points of the tail; bright green with sparse whitish hairs, and with faint darker green and yellowish lines running along body. Feeds on various grasses, especially cock's-foot and couch grassy.

Similar Species

Speckled Woods with orange patches on the wings are found in southern Europe; those with pale yellow patches in eastern, central and northern Europe and in Britain.

Flying Period

March–October.

The Speckled Wood is attracted to shady areas and is found all over Europe.

Other Browns

The Hermit

Wingspan: 42–68 mm. Female larger than male. Wings dark brown with a broken white band on fore wing, continuous white band on hind wing. Two dark spots on fore wing. Underside of fore wing similar, of hind wing (male) banded and mottled in white and brown, (female) mottled brown. Found in dry stony places from lowlands to 2000 m, central and southern Europe. Flies May–August. Caterpillar feeds on grasses, especially blue moor grass.

Other Browns

Black Satyr

Wingspan: 48–56 mm. Wings of male black with one white-centred eyespot on fore wing; female similar but dark brown, often with second spot on fore wing. Underside of fore wing (of both sexes) paler with similar spot(s), hind wing banded and mottled in brown and white. Found in dry stony slopes in Iberia, southern France and northern Italy. Flies July–August. Great Sooty Satyr male similar, female pale brown, both with two white-centred black spots on fore wing. Found in rocky hills in southern Europe.

Other Browns

♀

The Dryad

Wingspan: 54–70 mm. Wings of male dark brown with two blue-centred, black spots on fore wing, sometimes one on hind wing. Hind wings have scalloped margins. Undersides of wings similar but paler, hind wing may be darker at the base, lighter towards the margin. Female larger and paler, both on upper and lower sides, with larger spots. Found in grassy slopes, scrub and open woods, locally in central Europe. Flies July– August. Caterpillar feeds on grasses.

Other Browns

Woodland Brown

Wingspan: 50–56 mm. Wings light grey-brown, with a curved row of large, yellow-ringed eyespots towards the margin. Underside similar but with additional pale stripes either side of the eyespots. The inside stripe on the hind wing is white, all others yellow. Found in open woods from lowlands to 1000 m, locally across central Europe from France to southern Finland and Bulgaria. Absent from Britain. Flies June–July. Caterpillar feeds on grasses.

Monarch
Danaus plexippus

75–95 mm

Adult Characteristics

Wings tawny orange-brown with wide black margins spotted with white, and black veins. It has long fore wings. Undersides of wings similar in pattern but paler in colour.

Habitat and Distribution

Migrates far and wide in open country. Native to north America but now established and resident in the Canary Islands, and occasional vagrants reach Spain, Portugal, France and England.

Caterpillar Characteristics

Caterpillar transversely striped in white, yellow and black, with a pair of filaments at the head and rear. Feeds on milkweeds in north America, but on two native plants in the Canaries, one *Gossypium* and one *Euphorbia* species.

Similar Species

African Queen smaller, with black-bordered, light tawny-brown wings, white spots across fore-wing tips and three black spots on hind wing; resident in Canaries, sometimes seen in Greece.

Flying Period

Summer (N); all year (S).

The dramatic beauty of the Monarch butterfly is usually seen in north America, but occasionally it can be found in Europe.

Nettle-Tree Butterfly

Libythea celtis

34–44 mm

Adult Characteristics

Distinctive butterfly with long palps (mouthparts). Fore wings hooked but appear to be cut off at the tips, brown with orange patches and a single white spot. Hind wings similar but without the white spot.

Habitat and Distribution

Found in lowland areas in open countryside and open woods, around nettle-trees. Southern Europe from northern Spain and southern France to Greece and the Balkans, north to Hungary in eastern Europe; also migrating into the mountains in summer.

Caterpillar Characteristics

Caterpillar green with a white stripe along its back and a pink stripe on each side. Feeds on leaves of nettle-trees.

Similar Species

No similar species.

Flying Period

March–April & June–September.

♀

Small Skipper
Thymelicus flavus

26–30 mm

Adult Characteristics

Wings bright tawny orange with veins and margins outlined in black; male has a conspicuous black sex brand on each fore wing. Underside of fore wing pale tawny orange, fading to yellow-grey at wing tips and dark at base; of hind wing more greenish orange. Antenna-tip orange beneath.

Habitat and Distribution

Found in grassy places, meadows, woodland rides, roadside verges, up to 1800 m. Widespread throughout Europe, north to Denmark, Germany and Poland, and in England and Wales. Absent from Scandinavia, Scotland and Ireland.

Caterpillar Characteristics

Caterpillar has a large green head; its body is green with a dark line along the back and yellow-white stripes along the sides. It lives in a tube made of rolled grass leaf; and feeds on grasses, including Yorkshire fog and Timothy.

Similar Species

Essex Skipper is very similar but its antenna-tips are black beneath. **Lulworth Skipper** has yellow spots on fore wings.

Flying Period

June–August.

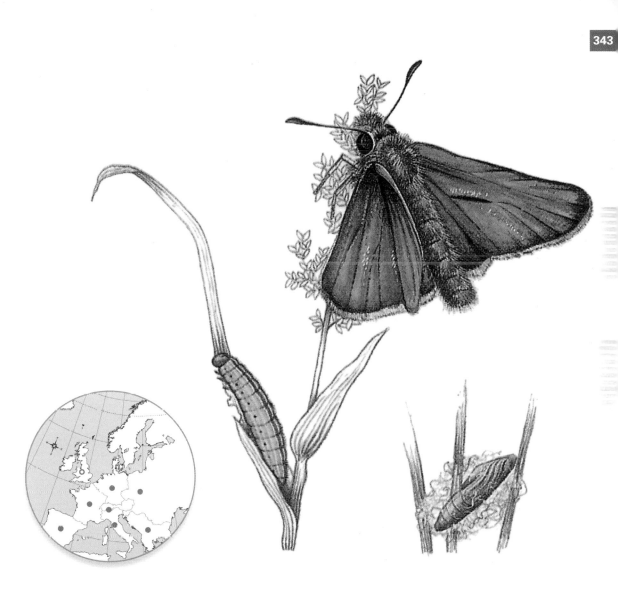

The Small Skipper flits around the meadows, woodlands and verges of much of Europe.

Large Skipper

Ochlodes venatus

28–34 mm

Adult Characteristics

Wings of male patchy orange with wide, dark-brown margins and a broad black sex brand on fore wing. Wings of female dark brown, with several orange patches on fore wing, fewer on hind wing. Underside pale orange and greenish, same pattern as upper side and with a black streak beneath sex brand in male.

Habitat and Distribution

Found in grassy places, meadows, woodland margins, waste places and near the sea, to 1800 m. Throughout much of Europe but absent from northern Scandinavia, Ireland and Scotland.

Caterpillar Characteristics

Caterpillar lives in a tube made from one or more rolled grass leaves, feeding on cock's-foot, false brome and other grasses. It has a large brown head and a blue-green body, with a dark line along the back and a yellow line along each side.

Similar Species

Silver-Spotted Skipper is similar but for the silver spots that it has on the undersides of the wing.

Flying Period

June–August.

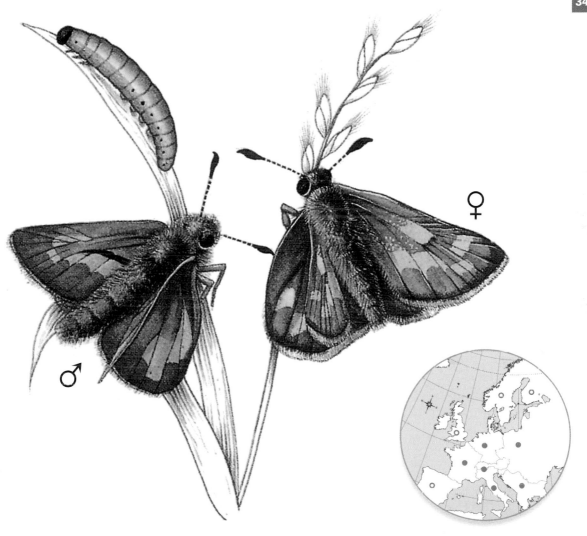

The Large Skipper is similar to the Silver-Spotted Skipper but for the sliver spots on the wing undersides.

Silver-Spotted Skipper

Hesperia comma

28–30 mm

Adult Characteristics

Wings patchy orange with wide, dark-brown margins and yellow spots near tips of fore wings; male has a broad black sex brand on each fore wing. Underside of fore wings yellow-brown near base, greenish with silvery spots towards the tips, of hind wings greenish with several silvery spots.

Habitat and Distribution

Found in grazed grassland, usually on chalk or limestone, from sea level to 2500 m, in local colonies across much of Europe. Absent from much of the far north, southern Spain and Italy, and from Ireland. Now only in southern England in Britain.

Caterpillar Characteristics

Caterpillar grub-like, with a large black head and a dull olive-green, rough-skinned body. It lives in a tent-like shelter formed of grass leaves and feeds on grasses, usually sheep's fescue.

Similar Species

The otherwise similar **Large Skipper** lacks the silver spots.

Flying Period

July–August.

The Silver-Spotted Skipper gets its name from the silver spots on the undersides of its wings.

Chequered Skipper

Carterocephalus palaemon

26–30 mm

Adult Characteristics

Wings dark brown and chequered with many orange-yellow spots. Underside orange-yellow, often tinged with green on hind wings, both wings with bands of pale yellow spots in same pattern as on upper side.

Habitat and Distribution

Found in open woods up to 1500 m, very locally across much of Europe, from France to the Balkans and northern Scandinavia. Absent from Denmark, southern Italy, most of Iberia. Probably extinct in England and only in western Inverness in Britain.

Caterpillar Characteristics

Caterpillar lives in a tube made from a rolled grass leaf. It is buff coloured with darker pinkish brown and white lines and a large head. Feeds on grasses, including purple moor grass and false brome.

Similar Species

Northern Chequered Skipper has yellow fore wings with brown spots, hind wings like Chequered Skipper. It flies in wooded valleys from northern Germany to Finland and Scandinavia.

Flying Period

June–July.

The Chequered Skipper is found across Europe, but only in very localized areas.

Large Chequered Skipper

32–38 mm

Heteropterus morpheus

Adult Characteristics

Wings plain dark brown but for three or four yellow spots near tip of each fore wing. Fringes chequered. Underside of fore wing also brown with yellow markings around the tip; of hind wing yellow with 12 large, whitish, dark-ringed spots and a dark band along inner margin.

Habitat and Distribution

Found in damp meadows and bogs, woodland clearings and rides. Scattered in small colonies locally in northern Spain, western and northern France, in Switzerland and northern Italy; also in Jersey. More widely distributed in Europe east of Germany.

Caterpillar Characteristics

Caterpillar lives in a tube made from a rolled grass leaf. It has a large pale, brown-striped head and a grey-white body with a dark line along the back and a white line along each side. Feeds on grasses, including false brome and purple moor grass.

Similar Species

With its distinctive wings, this skipper is unlikely to be mistaken for any other.

Flying Period

June–August.

Dingy Skipper
Erynnis tages

26–30 mm

Adult Characteristics

Fore wings dark brown crossed by white-powdered bands and rows of white spots; hind wings dark brown with bands of white spots. Underside golden brown with bands of less distinct cream-coloured spots near the margins. Male has fold in fore wing.

Habitat and Distribution

Found in downs and heaths, cliffs and dunes, roadside verges, often on calcareous soils, from sea level to 1800 m. Across Europe, north to southern Scandinavia; also in England and Wales, parts of Ireland and on some Scottish coasts.

Caterpillar Characteristics

Caterpillar is quite stout but tapers towards head and tail. It has a purplish-black head and grey-green body, covered with short white hairs. Found in a shelter of leaves on its foodplant, bird's-foot trefoil.

Similar Species

Only Inky Skipper, from the mountains of Greece and the Balkans, is similar and it lacks the white spots.

Flying Period

May–June (N); May–August (S).

The Dingy Skipper boasts white spots, a characteristic that separates it from the Inky Skipper.

Grizzled Skipper

Pyrgus malvae

22–26 mm

Adult Characteristics

Wings black, with irregular rows of distinct white spots and chequered black and white margins. Underside of fore wing grey-brown overlaid with white scales, of hind wing greenish or yellowish brown, both with white spots in a similar pattern to upper side; spots on hind wing larger than on upper side.

Habitat and Distribution

Found in flowery meadows and bogs, woodland rides and edges, from sea level to 2000 m across much of Europe, and in England and Wales. Absent from northern Scandinavia, Scotland and Ireland.

Caterpillar Characteristics

Caterpillar lives in a silk shelter beneath a leaf of its food plant, usually wild strawberry or one of the cinquefoils. It has a large black head and a yellow-green body, striped with darker brown and olive; it has many short pale hairs.

Similar Species

There are 13 similar related species in Europe, all difficult to tell apart.

Flying Period

April–June & July–August.

The Grizzled Skipper has 13 similarly related species in Europe, which can make it difficult to spot.

Red Underwing Skipper
Spialia sertorius

22–26 mm

Adult Characteristics

A variable species and the smallest European skipper. Wings dark brown to black with scattered white spots and a row of white spots near each margin, or with scattered yellow spots. Underside of fore wing dark grey, of hind wing brick red or red-brown, both with curved bands of pale whitish spots.

Habitat and Distribution

Found in dry rough places from lowlands to mountains, up to 1500 m. From Spain and Portugal locally through southern Europe to southern Germany, Austria and southern Italy.

Caterpillar Characteristics

Caterpillar lives in a shelter of leaves woven together with silk. It is short with a large head; its body is black with a yellowish stripe along the back and it has many long white hairs. It feeds on brambles, cinquefoils and burnet.

Similar Species

Hungarian Skipper is a related species, similar but for the olive-green colour of the hind wing underside. It flies in rough ground in eastern Europe, the Balkans and Greece.

Flying Period

April–June & July–August.

The underside of the hind wing of this butterfly is brick red, and so explains the species name of Red Underwing Skipper.

Mallow Skipper

Carcharodus alceae

26–34 mm

Adult Characteristics

Wings marbled brown, dark brown and grey, with glassy spots on fore wings. Hind wings have scalloped margins. Undersides paler brown with similar glassy spots on fore wing, and white or yellow spots on hind wing.

Habitat and Distribution

Found around flowery banks, on hills and slopes up to 1500 m. Throughout central and southern Europe, north to central France and Germany, east to the Ukraine.

Caterpillar Characteristics

Caterpillar lives in a shelter formed of leaves. It has a large black head with orange spots around the neck; the body is greenish-grey speckled with black and white and with many short whitish hairs. It feeds on mallow, marsh mallow and hibiscus.

Similar Species

Marbled Skipper has olive-brown wings marbled with olive-green and with white or glassy spots. It flies in dry chalky hills, mainly in southern Europe, more rarely north of the Alps.

Flying Period

April–August.

Other Skippers

Essex Skipper

Wingspan: 24–28 mm. Wings tawny orange-brown with black veins and margins; underside of fore wing pale orange-brown with yellow-grey wing tips and a dark streak in centre, of hind wing mainly yellow-grey. Male has black sex brand on fore wing. Underside of antenna-tip black. Found in meadows and grassy hillsides across Europe, north to southern Scandinavia; also in southern England. Flies June–August, often with the similar Small Skipper. Caterpillar feeds on various grasses.

Other Skippers

Lulworth Skipper

Wingspan: 22–26 mm. Wings dusky orange, fore wing with one indistinct yellow spot near centre and a curved series of similar yellow spots towards wing tip. Underside plain dusky yellow. Male has black sex brand on fore wing. Scattered in damp meadows and grassy places across southern and central Europe, only near coast in Devon and Dorset in Britain. Flies May–August. Caterpillar feeds on brome-grass and false brome-grass.

The Essex Skipper can be found throughout much of Europe, and is very similar to the Small Skipper both in appearance and in location.

Other Skippers

Large Grizzled Skipper

Wingspan: 28–32 mm. Wings dark grey-brown, with white spots on fore wing, large glassy mark and faint white spots on hind wing. Underside of hind wing olive-brown or green with large white marks. Found in flowery meadows in hills and mountains across southern and central Europe, rare further north to southern Scandinavia; absent from Britain. Flies June–August. Caterpillar feeds on cinquefoils, rock rose and brambles. Similar Safflower Skipper is found in similar places in central and southern Europe.

Other Skippers

Olive Skipper

Wingspan: 24–28 mm. Wings dark grey-brown with variable white spots on fore wing (sometimes almost absent, especially in female) and almost plain hind wings (spots if present very indistinct). Found in hills and mountains up to 2400 m, across much of southern and central Europe. Absent from northwest France, Holland and Britain. Flies June–August. Caterpillar feeds on lady's mantle and cinquefoils. One of several similar small skippers found in Europe.

Further Reading

Asher, J. (ed) et al, *The Millennium Atlas of Butterflies in Britain and Ireland*, Oxford University Press, 2001

Badger, D., *Butterflies*, Motorbooks International, 2006

Baran-Marescot, M., *Butterflies of the World*, Harry N. Abrams, Inc., 2006

Carter, D., *DK Handbook: Butterflies and Moths*, Dorling Kindersley Publishers Ltd., 2000

Chinery, M., *Butterflies (Collins Gem)*, Collins, 2004

Goodden, R. and Goodden, R., *Butterflies of Britain and Europe*, New Holland Publishers Ltd., 2002

Hofmann, H. and Marktanner, T., *Butterflies and Moths of Britain and Europe*, Collins, 1995

Landman, W., *Butterflies: Complete Encyclopedia*, Rebo International, 2006

Lewington, R., *Pocket Guide to the Butterflies of Great Britain and Ireland*, British Wildlife Publishing, 2003

Newland, D., *Discover Butterflies in Britain*, WILDGuides, 2006

Peterson, R.T., *First Guide to Caterpillars*, Houghton Mifflin (Trade), 1998

Porter, J., *Colour Identification Guide to Caterpillars of the British Isles*, Viking, 1997

Reader's Digest, *Field Guide to the Butterflies and Other Insects of Britain*, Reader's Digest, 2001

Sandved, K.B. and Cassie, B., *World of Butterflies*, Bulfinch Press, 2004

Sterry, P. and Mackay, A., *Butterflies and Moths*, Dorking Kindersley Publishers Ltd., 2004

Tampion, J. and Tampion, M., *How to Attract Butterflies to Your Garden*, Guild of Master Craftsman Publications Ltd., 2003

Thomas, J.A., *Butterflies of the British Isles*, Hamlyn, 1992

Tolman, T., *Butterflies of Europe*, Princeton University Press, 2002

Tomlinson, D., *Britain's Butterflies*, WILDGuides, 2002

Picture Credits

All photographs courtesy of NHPA/Photoshot: Alan Barnes: 24–5, 30–1, 52–3, 108–9, 138–9, 154–5, 198–9, 206–7, 214–5, 226–7, 230–1, 238–9, 246–7, 262–3, 266–7, 352–3, 356–7, 362–3; Simon Booth: 80–1, 272–3; Gerry Cambridge: 110–1, 122–3; Laurie Campbell: 38–9, 118–9, 170–1, 242–3, 282–3, 292–3, 302–3, 314–5; Stephen Dalton: 42–3; 56–7, 68–9, 252–3, 256–7, 320–1, 330–1, 344–5, 366–7; Martin Garwood: 88–9, 92–3, 96–7, 100–1, 174–5, 188–9, 288–9, 296–7, 324–5, 370–1; Paul Hermansen: 162–3; T. Kitchen & Hurst: 338–9; Chris Mattison: 376–7; Mirko Stelzner: 348–9; Robert Thompson: 34–5, 46–7, 64–5, 74–5, 128–9, 134–5, 144–5, 150–1, 166–7, 178–9, 194–5, 210–1, 222–3, 234–5, 276–7, 310–1; Dave Watts: 60–1; Werner Zepf: 300–1; Daniel Zupanc: 182–3.

Index and Checklist

All species in Roman type are illustrated.
Keep a record of your sightings by ticking the boxes.